MACDONALD COMPUTER MONOGRAPHS

General Editor: Stanley Gill, M.A., Ph.D.,

Professor of Computing Science,
Imperial College, London

BASIC MACHINE PRINCIPLES

BASIC MACHINE PRINCIPLES

J. K. ILIFFE

*International Computers
and Tabulators Limited*

MACDONALD: LONDON

First published in 1968 by
Macdonald & Co. (Publishers) Ltd.
49-50 Poland Street, London, W.1.
Made and printed in Great Britain by
Hazell Watson & Viney Ltd., Aylesbury, Bucks

CONTENTS

PREFACE

This book is concerned with the definition of a computer system from the programming point of view. Its primary interest will be to logical designers and programmers who occupy themselves with the boundary between the 'hard' and 'soft' parts of a computer. However, decisions reached at this level have far-reaching effects, and it is expected that their implications will also interest computer engineers and users who depend indirectly on the logical ability and speed of general purpose machines, and seek to employ them efficiently.

The machine definition is presented in terms of a symbolic language, whose fundamental origins are reflected in the name 'Basic Language'. The hard and fast practical requirements are embodied in the Basic Machine, and the language itself is realised by an integrated system of stored programs and logic which together constitute the Basic Language Machine, or BLM.

A relatively long and expensive piece of research of this nature could not be undertaken without the support of many colleagues and friends, whose help I salute. It is also a pleasure to acknowledge the timely support of the Ministry of Technology Advanced Computer Technology Project for the development of programs on the experimental Basic Machine, from which the present work is partly derived.

April 1968   J. K. Iliffe
Advance Research and Development Division,
I.C.T. Ltd., Stevenage, Herts

1

GENERAL PRINCIPLES

The ultimate objective in designing a computer is to see it produced and applied effectively to current scientific and data-processing problems, and quickly adapted to an expanding range of activities. Modern production methods, and the magnitude of investment in programming systems, both require that the design principles be common to a large number of machines of varying capacity and speed, and that they remain valid over a timespan in which new system components may, judging by recent history, be invented with striking regularity. It follows that the search for fundamental principles of design is of economic importance as well as being a challenging pursuit in its own right.

Perhaps the most fundamental principle, to which all complex devices owe their existence, is that of dividing the computer into a number of component parts, and defining each by stating how it responds to the actions of its neighbours. The usual method of engineering design is to begin by constructing a theoretical model of each component, and agreeing that it meets the functional requirements of the system. The engineer can then use his skill to find an acceptable compromise between cost and performance, provided the rules laid down by the model are not violated. If the model is well chosen, a large number of alternative ways of implementing it will present themselves, and the number of uses to which it can be put will increase accordingly.

An equivalent way of analysing a computer system is in terms of the boundaries or 'interfaces' between each component and its neighbours. Depending on one's technical point of view, any boundary is capable of assuming prime importance and characterising the machine as an advance on its predecessors. In the current generation of computers, for example, one might say that the 'standard interface' between the central part of the system and the peripheral data-handling devices is the most important concept to have been developed. In the present book, we shall be concerned with the boundary between a central processing unit and the directly addressable storage complex, i.e. with the way programs are held in the store when being obeyed. It was across this boundary that engineers and programmers faced one another in the early days of

1

computers, and the tradition of introducing a computer by defining its machine language dies hard, even though most contemporary programmers would probably view such information with disdain.

However, the Basic Language Machine is not introduced in this way for reasons of sentiment. By means of assembly programs a second 'boundary' is normally presented to programmers in the form of a *symbolic input language*, from whose expressions machine language programs can be generated. Closer inspection reveals that this is not really a boundary at all, since the language is defined in terms of the binary programs it generates, and there is no effective way of preventing a programmer from using the generated coding inconsistently, either by accident or deliberately. It is one of the main arguments of this book that the symbolic input language should indeed be the primary interface between programmers and central processing units, but that it should be defined independently of the binary machine language. It is easy to see that a conventional machine design cannot satisfy this requirement, and we shall describe a machine which does have the desired characteristics. In fact, we shall do no more than apply the principle already noted: that one should define a component of the computer (in this case, the set of expressions of its primitive control language) by what it *does*, rather than by what it *is*. Although the immediate consequences of redrawing a boundary now well submerged in the total computer system may appear to be small, there seems little doubt that their effects will be felt eventually throughout the software complex, and its method of manufacture.

In the present chapter, we continue the examination of first principles, and isolate certain concepts which one would hope to be recognised in a programming system. The conclusions are by no means entirely new, and we are able (in Chapter 2) to examine certain practical embodiments of some of the same basic principles. Thus armed with *a priori* argument and observation we proceed in Chapter 3 and 4 to characterise the central processor hardware and input language of the Basic Language Machine. Finally some of the implications of such a system and its immediate extensions are considered.

1.1 The engineering model

Most computers of today are said to follow the 'von Neumann' model of central processor design, after the pioneering study presented by Burks, Goldstine, and von Neumann[1]. In fact, the von Neumann machine used what we would call a 'single accumulator' scheme of operations, which was fairly quickly superseded by the multiple accumulator predecessors of present-day systems, taking better advantage of the observed patterns of access to data. In other respects, too, gradual refinement of the model has taken place: the individual operations performed at each computing step have been allowed to vary; the size of memory has ranged from around 1000 words up to 200 000 words or more; the size of words has ranged from six bits to sixty-four; the simple rule of obeying 'one step at a time' has been relaxed to allow calculation to proceed in parallel with transfers of information to and from the memory, of which in many machines the programmer must keep an account; and the emergence of a permanent set of 'system routines' has insulated the user from the vagaries of the slower parts of the computer system.

Perhaps the most important characteristic of the von Neumann model, however, remains the concept of a single 'linear store' addressed by consecutive location numbers (usually from 0 to m, a power of 2), in which instructions are not distinguished from data. Early descriptions of coding techniques stressed the importance and difficulty of this concept[2], but although after the introduction of instruction modification it was no longer an essential feature of an order code, no attempts appear to have been made to eliminate it for another twelve years[3].

If we examine a selection of mathematical and data-handling problems (as they arise in a service bureau, for example), it is extremely unlikely that their data and instruction storage requirements will fall easily into the mould of the linear store. The more general the expression of the problem, the less likely are they to do so. If the quantity of data is liable to fluctuate, enough room must be left for its expansion to maximum size; if the course of calculation is complex, it becomes an increasing burden on the programmer to ensure that the required routines and data are in position at each phase of calculation, and the help offered by the system often leads to awkward programming restrictions. We shall consider some of the problems of store assignment in the next chapter, but for the moment it is sufficient to comment that the conventional means of translating and obeying programs act as a filtering mechanism, admitting to the computer only those problems whose solution justifies the cost of translation into a rigid store structure.

We should not be surprised, therefore, that efforts to find a computer model appropriate to modern applications usually end up with the imprint of the von Neumann machine. It might indeed be supposed that the expense of current programming systems precludes a radical departure in design, and that the rapid advance of technology should simply be exploited to do the same jobs in the same way, but more cheaply. It is, of course, a prime requirement that any new design should meet current standards of programming as efficiently as possible. The common 'problem-oriented languages' conveniently express the structure of conventional machines and some of the problems to which they are suited, and the investment in, for example, Fortran or Cobol programming can be assured by carrying such

3

standards into future machines. As a method of design, however, it is clear that starting with conventional assumptions about the nature of storage and instructions, one can do no more than reinforce the filtering mechanism already established: more problems may find their way through, but the mixture will remain as before.

What evidence have we that conventional computers are near the limit of adaptability? Surely they are general purpose machines, and can be used to solve any problem? In a mathematical sense this is true, but the point we have been making is that the cost may be so high that *economic* solution is impossible. Most programmers can find examples from their own experience in which the necessity of fitting a problem into a linear store has proved either difficult or expensive, though we should take note of the fact that professional programmers have been subjected to the same process of artificial selection as their problems. It is the unprofessional user who is more likely to complain of the restrictive rules of the language he has to employ and of the 'moronic' behaviour of the machine when a situation arises for which he has not provided, and he might reasonably ask whether we need to perpetuate such a state of affairs.

An example

To illustrate some of the issues involved, let us consider the following simple problem. Assume that certain traffic surveys are made by stopping all private cars travelling in one or both directions on a stretch of road and recording for each traveller:

(a) the name of the starting point of his journey;
(b) the name of the destination; and
(c) the number of passengers.

The information so obtained is presented to the computer in records of a prescribed format. It is required to write a program to summarise the result of the survey, by printing for each observed starting point and destination the number of cars with none, one, two, three, or more passengers.

We proceed as follows. Since the starts and destinations are not given, they must be constructed by the program in the form of two tables of names. Let S be the table of starting points and D the table of destinations in a particular survey. The tables are initially 'empty', and are filled up as new names are read from the input records. We denote the number of computer words assigned to S by '$Length (S)$', and similarly for D. It is assumed that one computer word is sufficient for each name. Then the tables can be used to reduce each record to a pair of non-negative integers (s, d), corresponding to the positions in the tables of names of the start and destination, and a number n of passengers, which is assumed not to exceed four.

For each (s,d) there is to be stored a table of five numbers sum-

4

marising the passenger load. If we arrange to store the summary tables in a single block B, then the table for any (s,d) can be arranged to start at position k relative to the first word of B, where:

$$k = 5 * s * Length(D) + 5 * d \tag{1·1·1}$$

(Note that the 'relative position' of the *first* word of each table is taken to be *zero*.) The task of the program is then read to each sample, obtain (s,d) by searching S and D, evaluate k, and, by reference to n, add one to the appropriate cell in B. Finally, the summary of results is to be printed out.

The essence of the problem is the variability in the amount of data to be stored. If we assume *Length* (D) will not exceed 100, and similarly for S, then B extends to 50 000 locations, most of which are probably unused. By assuming not more than 1000 pairs (s,d) in use, it is possible to set up an intermediate table A replacing the above relation for k by some arbitrary allocation of indices, i.e. in the kth entry of A is stored an (s,d) pair, and the evaluation $(1·1·1)$ of k is accomplished by scanning A. The space required by A now amounts to 1000 words, but the summary table B is reduced from 50 000 to 5000.

Thus, by making certain assumptions about the nature of the problem, it has been reduced to manageable proportions. Since it isn't quite the same as the original, the traffic engineer will have to take note of some restrictions when using it—he may later ask for another 'solution' to the same problem, with another set of restrictions. Fig. 1 indicates the main storage blocks and their disposition in a linear store. Shaded regions indicate store locations of variable extent, which would normally have to be fixed before calculation commenced. It can be seen that the logic implied by the mechanism of store control is already more complex than the arithmetic part, a state of affairs also present in more realistic programs. Many trained programmers doubtless view this as the natural order of things, and would easily be able to offer variations on the method of solution, based on different assumptions. Yet the problem is unchanged, and in view of the cost of defining and programming a solution, it is sensible to enquire whether all the assumptions are justified by consequent saving of machine and human effort. We shall attempt to show in succeeding chapters that they are not.

1.2 Basic objectives

The first requirement of the von Neumann model was to characterise the physical components of a computer system in such a way that it could be programmed. The addressable store, for example, was presented in just the way that existing storage techniques and selection mechanisms could be made to work. However, as many contemporary machines demonstrate, it is no longer necessary for

5

the machine boundary to be determined by crude physical characteristics, and amongst the most important considerations are the mathematical natures of the problems to be solved, and of the process of calculation itself. The first approach to the machine order code should therefore be 'from the outside', working inwards until an economical hardware interface can be defined. There are, of course, many abstract treatments of the subject of calculation or 'computability', but their objectives are of little practical consequence.

Fig. 1. A 'linear' program store

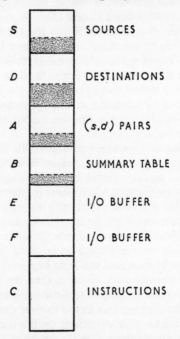

S	SOURCES
D	DESTINATIONS
A	(s,d) PAIRS
B	SUMMARY TABLE
E	I/O BUFFER
F	I/O BUFFER
C	INSTRUCTIONS

In order to compete in speed with existing machines, it is necessary to prescribe elementary computational steps of at least their order of complexity, and one cannot afford to ignore the fact that arrays of data objects must somehow be represented in a finite physical store, and account must be taken of the practical aspects of writing, developing, and running programs. It is from this starting point that a definite set of objectives can be formulated.

Structure of programs

From a mathematical viewpoint, the problem we have just considered involves the manipulation of a *matrix M* of elements $M_{s,d}$, each of which is a *vector* of five integers. The relationship

6

between individual parts of a program is termed its *structure*. Elementary mathematics uses structural terms ('matrix', 'vector') and formulae ('$M_{s,d}$') which are convenient for giving simple examples, but not sufficiently expressive for the range of programs run on computers, and we shall be concerned to extend them. The structure recognised by a von Neumann type of computer, however, is no more than a single vector containing data and instructions. It is the task of a programmer to reduce the problem to linear form, which he does by *absorbing* the structure into the logic of the program. This can be done either by restricting the variables of the problem in such a way that the absorption rules become particularly simple, and realisable by conventional hardware, or by assuming full responsibility for storage allocation in the program itself, using stored routines to 'interpret' data accesses. On one hand, Fortran provides the classic example; at the other extreme we find list processing languages. In order to be both unrestrictive and fast, it is essential to consider a third possibility, that the 'hardware' recognise the inherent structure of programs, i.e. for program logic to be freed from absorbed structure, and for the recognition to be carried out at high speed relative to a core store cycle.

The development of 'system programming' for multiprogram machines presents problems which cannot be solved efficiently by absorption. Each program on such a machine, being written independently, must assume a linear store of its own, 'addressed' from 0 to an m depending on the program. In actual core store, each program may be assigned to a range of consecutive locations, within which the program's 'addresses' are used as relative indices. The situation is remarkably similar to that depicted in Fig. 1, except that each separate storage block represents a distinct program. The system program sees all others as a set of vectors whose total demand for core store space varies unpredictably, and which must therefore be satisfied dynamically, i.e. as it occurs. The first step is to give each program an implied base or 'datum' address b which, held in a fast-access register, automatically modifies each program 'address' and checks to see that the limit m has not been exceeded; combining m with b this gives an exact description of the position of a program in store, in the form of a datum-limit word:

m	b	Datum-Limit Word
Limit	Datum	

It is precisely by recognising such elementary descriptions in the hardware that the fluctuating demand for storage is satisfied. Since their use is implicit, they have no effect on coding techniques within a single program. The system program itself must have access to the datum-limit words, so that it can reorganise store dynamically: if a 'user' program is moved to a new position starting at base b' in store then b is changed to b' in its datum-limit word, m is unchanged, and no alteration is necessary in the program itself. By bringing the use of datum-limit words into the normal programming domain, structural qualities of users' programs may also be represented. It must be evident, however, that a datum-limit word could not be freely manipulated by the programmer in the same way as binary data, since then the independent structural quality would be lost.

An examination of system programming techniques illustrates some of the implications of adopting a nonlinear store structure. Provided each program is strictly confined to its own region of store, it is a relatively simple matter to ensure that the correct datum-limit register is loaded before execution, and that the datum values are adjusted to accord with any movement of the program in the core memory. If one program has to communicate with the store of another—for example, a system routine performing a task for a user—it has to address one store region for instructions and another for data. An implicit datum-limit word is no longer sufficient, and must be supplemented by a method of *explicit* selection associated with a privileged or 'system' mode of operation. If the system mode also allows datum-limit values to be changed, then the possibility of consistent checking of structure by hardware is lost, and the system programmer must devise and adhere to *software* conventions which preserve the conceptual structure of the store. In this way, system programming has tended to develop as a separate discipline, requiring not only highly skilled programmers but also exclusive use of the computer system for debugging runs, even though only a very small part of the program may logically require privileged facilities.

The plea to be made here is for *consistency* in the engineering model. The von Neumann machine has this quality, which makes it impossible to 'break through' the rules to control the machine in any other way. However, we have seen that for certain problems, and for multiprogram control in particular, the linear storage model is unsuitable. Since the wider the class of users which can be satisfied, the more valuable the model, we might formulate as a design objective that the conceptual store structure presented by the engineering model should include the common requirements both of system programming and of conventional data structures, in the hope of narrowing the gulf which now exists between 'system' and 'user' modes of operation.

We have attempted to justify the explicit recognition of program structure on the grounds that the running programs will be more general or more efficient than they would be in a linear store, and hence that the investment in programming and machine time is more profitable. There is one other consideration which weighs heavily in favour of a structured store in certain situations, namely that of program development in its widest sense, of which 'on-line interaction' is a special case. Here again one is dealing with an unpredictable store structure, even though in the final running program the structure may easily be absorbed to give a linear form. A partially developed program consists of several blocks of instructions and data, each subject to correction when errors are discovered. As the problem specification becomes more precise, additions are made, temporary pieces of coding are removed, exceptional conditions are detected and dealt with, the presentation of results is negotiated with the problem analyst, and so on. All these activities can demand a change in structure, and if the program cannot be run without being linearised, each change implies at least a partial reassembly, by no means a trivial operation for the system. The price is paid in machine loading and programmers' service in both the batch-processing and interactive environments.

Thus, if the engineering model recognises program segment structure, program alteration may be greatly simplified. We should add to the general objectives of the model that it accomplish this, together with providing for data structures as already noted. An incidental and important benefit from consistent structural interpretation is that programming errors are detected sooner than in a linear store, since the structural description implies more stringent limit tests. It also follows that the state of a program can be reported to the user in terms of its structure, with the result that fault diagnosis is simplified. If we take the view that many programs spend a large proportion of their existence in the development phase, and some never graduate from it, the significance of retaining structure in the model must clearly be very great.

Control

Having examined some of the principal difficulties of the linear store, it is appropriate to turn to the control elements, to see if comparable disadvantages can be found. In the von Neumann machine, control is exercised by a single sequence of instructions, each of which performs an operation on specified operands before passing to the next. By making the instruction format explicit, it is possible to calculate the position of an instruction in store and to obey a conditional or unconditional jump to it. Also, as already noted, the ability exists to operate on instructions arithmetically, and may be exploited to achieve special logical effects.

The first observation to make is that if the memory is characterised in some nonlinear way, then the instruction code must be adapted to take account of the fact, in the selection of both operands and instructions. The exceptional nature of datum-limit words as operands has already been noted. Secondly, it is precisely the ability to calculate the position of instructions and perform arithmetic on them that prevents a program from being readily translated from one machine to another (arithmetic and addressing functions are more easily simulated). Since the usefulness of the model is partly determined by the accumulation of programs written for it, the greater the freedom of the engineer to adapt the instruction code to new situations, without breaking the rules, the better. It is therefore appropriate to take as a design objective the specification of instructions in such a way that they can be translated readily from one format to another without human intervention, i.e. by not making explicit the exact form in which instructions are stored for execution.

Thirdly, we note that for nearly all practical programming purposes, instructions and data are described by a symbolic assembly language which allows full control of machine facilities. If the definition of standard instructions can be made in a similar symbolic form, then an important practical step will have been made towards the use of the machine, but it should be noted that the essence of the symbolic language as a *system component* is the ability to control the formation of all instruction sequences, and to incorporate checks which otherwise would be carried out dynamically. For example, it can be arranged that all possible control paths within a segment are completely monitored during translation, and there is no need to carry out validity checks during execution. The *mnemonic* value of the input language is of rather less importance, especially as it is easily changed without affecting the machine design. In Chapter 4, advantage is taken of this fact in simplifying the presentation of Basic Language.

Parallelism

In the execution of sequences of instructions, there are many instances of contemporary machines using parallel control in order to achieve high performance. A sufficient condition for the initiation of independent parallel sequences is that they operate on distinct sets of variable data. At the level of central registers, it is possible for the machine logic to check that the condition is satisfied; it is desirable to have a register organisation for which such checks are relatively simple and effective. At the system level, any two independent programs can clearly be run in parallel or in any other time relationship to suit the economics of the system. The special case of peripheral transfers is one in which a physical interlock is required, because the two processes involved are not independent: it has to be decided whether such a mechanism should be 'brought to the surface' in the engineering model and, indeed, whether the expression of local parallelism is a useful feature of the instruction code.

Clearly, if system programming is itself to form part of the model, then it must be possible to initiate parallel processes. Also, if certain forms of simulation are to be programmed, it may be convenient to express them as parallel activities, quite apart from material benefits in performance which may follow. It has already been postulated that some structural data representation be allowed; it is natural to conclude that in the first approximation the structure *should* allow for the isolation of data sets during parallel processing, automatically applying interlocks when access is disallowed, and resolving problems of 'ownership' where the sharing of information is permitted. It is this requirement which imposes rather stringent conditions on the sort of structural qualities which can be recognised by the computer system.

Elementary operands

A computation step generally consists of performing an operation on one or two operands taken from specified positions in the store, and placing the result in a third position (possibly one of the first two). The finite range of numbers is augmented by the possibility of choosing from alternative representations within a single order code. The choice of floating point, integer, fixed point, fractional, and decimal representations of varying precision is commonly available in the form of different 'types' of operand, the distinction between types being made in the choice of operation, rather than in the data itself. If there are, say, four types recognised by the computer, and six elementary operations between them, some 96 inter-register functions are possible, and if either operand may be in core storage the number rises to 384. The conventional procedure of encoding type as part of the function would imply the provision of a 9-bit field for arithmetic function selection alone. In practice the list of functions is severely (and somewhat arbitrarily) curtailed to make more efficient use of instruction space. However, the fundamental disadvantage of dissociating type selection from data remains: that it is left to the programmer to ensure that the correct function is used on each data representation, that conversion from one representation to another is programmed where necessary, that arguments presented to subroutines assume the correct representation, and so on. If the rules are not observed, then some curious arithmetic results are produced, which can be regarded as errors in by far the majority of instances.

An alternative approach is to associate type with data at all times. Provided the type coding distinguishes address from number representations, there remain only the arithmetic operations to be selected by the instruction, further resolution being effected by the data types. The space required for function digits in the instructions is thereby minimised, and the kinds of problems referred to in the previous paragraph are eliminated in exchange for the minority of instances in which curious arithmetic results are required, which can be achieved in other ways.

11

It appears at first sight that whatever is gained by simplifying the encoding of instructions is counterbalanced by associating two or more type bits with every piece of data; in a machine where the data elements themselves may require only an 8-bit representation, an appreciable storage overhead could be inferred. As a practical observation, however, data elements occur predominantly in finite, ordered *sets* with the same representation, e.g., character strings, sets of integers, etc., so if we can arrange for the type information to be provided as part of the 'set description', the extra storage requirement is very small indeed. The consideration of machine operations thus leads back to the description of program structures, which we have taken as a basic objective of the engineering model, and it follows that the source of type information should be the structural description itself, i.e. a generalisation of the datum-limit word.

Apart from distinguishing different data representations, some form of type coding is necessary to discriminate between data, instructions and addresses. It has been proposed to conceal binary instructions from the user; therefore, any attempt to read or write them must be detected and treated as an error. Similarly, an address, which in general will contain datum and limit information, must be treated differently from numerical data. It happens that the same pattern of coding which distinguishes one numerical data type from another can also be used in this more general sense. We can immediately see the 'structure' of a program taking shape in the form of sets of instructions, sets of data, and sets of addresses: *their* interconnections remain to be determined by considerations of problem and system economics.

Escape actions

The exact specification of even a relatively simple computer is a difficult task, rarely achieved in advance of its construction. Complete definition of the order code of a modern computer system is not only impossible in practice but also undesirable at the hardware design level, simply because the resolution of many of its actions may depend on the installation, the operating environment, or even the program being obeyed at a given instant. This does not mean that the primary definition of an 'ADD' function can vary from one instant to the next. The constant part of the order code must be sufficiently comprehensive to include elementary arithmetic and logical functions, data storage, retrieval, and control sequencing operations, so that most programs can be written on the assumption that no exceptional conditions arise. If, however, an event such as numerical overflow, or an invalid address, or an information transfer failure is detected, recourse must generally be made to stored instructions to complete the function interpretation.

It is the task of the hardware to detect exceptional conditions and enter the appropriate interpretive routine. In the Basic Machine, the terms 'escape action' and 'escape routine' are used in this sense. If the escape action is slow, then its utility is confined to rare events such as program errors or peripheral failures. On the other hand, if the selection of an escape routine is fast, and its parameters are readily accessible, then the escape mechanism becomes a practical means of completing the definition of the order code.

It will be seen that extensive use is made of escape actions in the Basic Machine. They are employed by the store control routines to effect temporary 'lock-out' of shared data, to make automatic use of secondary storage media, and for various monitoring and sequence control purposes. They are used in the detection of invalid or 'undefined' data, and for resolving conflicts between uncommon combinations of operand types. They can also lead directly to functional (as opposed to numerical) data definitions, which may be used heavily in certain contexts. For these reasons, it is desirable to make allowance for fast escape actions in the machine design, and to formalise their use in the input language. It is also important to note that since the escape routine may be supplied by the user *or* by one of the resident system routines, a flexible system of addressing is essential. The explicit recognition of program structure meets this requirement.

1.3 Primary consequences

In the Basic Machine, a third component of stored information— the structural description—is added to the two with which we are already familiar, i.e. instructions and data. It might be argued that existing 'high level' languages have to a large extent already achieved the objectives of the Basic Machine. They are certainly symbolic, they appear to recognise data structures and different types of elementary operands, and a start has been made on the initiation of parallel processes and escape actions. Would it not be possible to devise a programming language, with all the necessary facilities, to run on a conventional machine? The brief answer is that it would, but it would be unduly expensive to run. Existing compilers only 'recognise' structure by virtue of restrictions on input languages which enable it to be absorbed during translation, or by the use of interpretive (and therefore slow) execution modes, or, as we shall see in Chapter 2, by making a rough job of the translation, leaving the programmer to protect himself from errors.

Provided the information units are large in comparison with a stored word, interpretive evaluation of structure is satisfactory. Thus, file handling routines and matrix arithmetic 'packages' have been in existence from the early days of computers. Any unique properties of the Basic Machine must stem from its use of hardware for detailed structural interpretation, and from this it follows that

13

its unique advantages must arise from speed of interpretation, and its disadvantages from the apparent lack of flexibility and cost.

We may summarise the expected benefits in the following way:

(a) *Versatility*. The information structure representing a program may be chosen at each step to correspond closely with that assumed by the programmer in his description of the problem, down to an information unit of the order of a character field or word. The class of problems which can be tackled economically is larger than for conventional (i.e. von Neumann) machines, since it includes those of variable structure.

(b) *Exact representation*. The input language can be obeyed strictly, in the sense that limit checks are determined by the individual parts of the data structure, not by the program area as a whole. Hence an important class of programming errors can be detected automatically, and diagnostic reports can make use of structural information to provide intelligible output. It is therefore to be expected that the detection and correction of program errors will be cheaper on a Basic Machine than on others.

(c) *System integration*. Basic Language manipulates both scalar and nonscalar quantities. It allocates storage dynamically, i.e. in response to commands executed in the course of a program, or in response to system demands, the space allocated to a program may be increased, decreased or redistributed over the available storage media. It may be used to control time-shared or parallel processes. It therefore has the essential features of an operating language, and in fact combines into one the commands of a symbolic language, and the directives of an operating system. The system itself can take advantage of program structures to integrate primary and secondary levels of storage, and to control asynchronous processes, without requiring additional hardware.

(d) *Concealment of non-numerical coding*. Machine code is protected in the form in which it is held for execution. Neither instructions nor addresses may be used as data, and their form may be varied to optimise machine performance in certain areas, e.g. extreme ends of a machine range, without sacrificing the investment in Basic Language programs.

(e) *Advanced applications*. The Basic Machine makes feasible coding techniques which have hitherto been uneconomical, and remain largely unexplored. By developing the use of type coding in language design and data monitoring, by exploiting the use of escape actions, and by adapting the structural representation to meet system as well as user requirements, it is expected that a set of techniques offering significant advantages over existing practice will be developed.

Against these arguments can be put the costs of maintaining a structure and addressing through it:

14

(f) *Running costs.* Since data structure may be held in the store at execution time, extra store accesses are sometimes required to obtain a particular item of information, where in a linear store one might address it directly.

(g) *Initial costs and overheads.* Setting up the structure and controlling a relatively complicated storage allocation system impose further overheads, and may reduce overall system performance.

(h) *Restrictions on programming.* Although it has been suggested that by allowing the programmer to use datum-limit information he gains a degree of flexibility, it is possible to argue that the necessary limitation on their use actually deprives him of some facility he previously enjoyed. Indeed, any attempt to formalise programming concepts (such as type or block structure) to the extent that they can be recognised by the 'hard' part of the system is sure to lead to protests from people who prefer to put their own interpretations on data. This is probably the main objection to programming in a high-level language of any sort. In the present instance, however, it will be seen that most conventional techniques can still be applied, where the programmer is willing to accept *their* limitations. Legitimate protest can only arise if, in fact, the greater generality of a Basic Machine leads to decreased system performance.

The above criticisms and the claimed advantages of the Basic Language Machine obviously require careful examination, and are the subject of a continuing research program. Although a full account of the arguments is outside the scope of this book, we shall return briefly to them in the last chapter.

2

SOME RELATED SYSTEMS

In the Basic Language Machine the store can be described, to a first approximation, as a 'tree structure'. The conceptual storage elements are grouped together in sets of various types. Data and instruction sets constitute the major part, but they are positioned relative to one another by the structural information, i.e. the generalised form of datum-limit word, for which the term 'codeword' is used[4]. Codewords are also grouped into sets, and they occupy the 'branch points' of the tree. It is characteristic of the structure that each set has exactly one codeword, and each codeword, with one exception, is a member of a set with a codeword at a 'higher level' in the tree. The exception is the *principal* codeword of the structure, which occupies the highest level. The idea of 'level' is used to indicate the number of steps necessary to reach a given element from the principal codeword, by way of the intermediate branch points—the greater the number, the *lower* the level. (The reader will note that in Basic Machine vegetation trees grow either downwards or sideways from left to right.)

In diagramatic form, a codeword can be represented as:

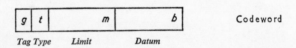

In the Basic Machine, the *Limit* value of any set is one less than its *Length*. It can be seen that two fields have been added to the datum and limit information. The primary requirement of the type t is to describe the elements in the set referred to by m and b. For consistency with the development of Chapter 3, the following type codes are used here:

type $t = 0$ refers to binary numeric elements
  $t = 4$ refers to instructions
  $t = 8$ refers to codewords

It is not always the case that a codeword refers to an explicitly defined and accessible set; in the course of building a tree structure, for example, many codewords may be left 'undefined' until a late

16

stage of calculation, and any attempts to use them for explicit data access must be monitored. To distinguish such situations, the tag g is given the following values:

tag $g = 1$ if the codeword requires 'escape' interpretation;
$g = 2$ if the codeword is interpreted as above.

Further tag codes will be introduced in the next chapter. Escape actions are illustrated by the systems discussed below.

It is sensible to omit b from diagrams, since it is only significant to the privileged store control routines, and to introduce an arrow pointing from a codeword to the first element of the set it defines, represented by a single block:

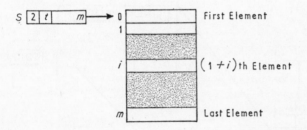

Set elements are distinguished by their *index values* (written along-side), which are non-negative integers, either constants or variables to be assigned in the course of calculation. Where no ambiguity can arise, it is permissible to use expressions such as 'the number (or instruction) i' to denote the value of the element (or instruction) at the ith index position, or 'the codeword S' to denote the value of the codeword at the Sth position. But since a codeword can describe a set of elements, it is also permissible to use 'the *set S*', or 'the *array S*' or 'the *program S*' to refer to the entire substructure based on the codeword at S.

Fig. 2 represents a hypothetical and much simplified system store consisting of two programs whose highest level codewords P and Q reside in the set defined by the principal codeword U. It is supposed that P consists of a single block of instructions, so this corresponds closely with the von Neumann concept of a linear program area. On the other hand, Q is a structured program consisting of six components, and the codeword Q (tag 2, type 8) refers to a codeword set of six elements ($m = 5$). The program Q has been chosen to represent the store used in the example of Chapter 1 (p. 6), with which it should be compared. Note that one component (index 4) refers to a pair of codewords, E and F, defining the input/output buffers, which are at a lower level than the remaining sets.

The reasons for starting with a tree structure should now become apparent. Firstly, it is a simple and commonly applicable concept, which does not require elaborate system engineering to implement. Secondly, it is a generalisation of a linear store, and one can expect to benefit wherever possible from the store assignment techniques developed for conventional machines. Thirdly, it has the desirable properties of being virtually infinite in capacity, and variable in form. Lastly, it provides relatively easily for the sort of separability required by parallel processes, and the substructures have the same general properties as their parent, e.g. each substructure has a 'principal codeword' with a tree structure of variable level dependent on it.

Fig. 2. Tree-structured program

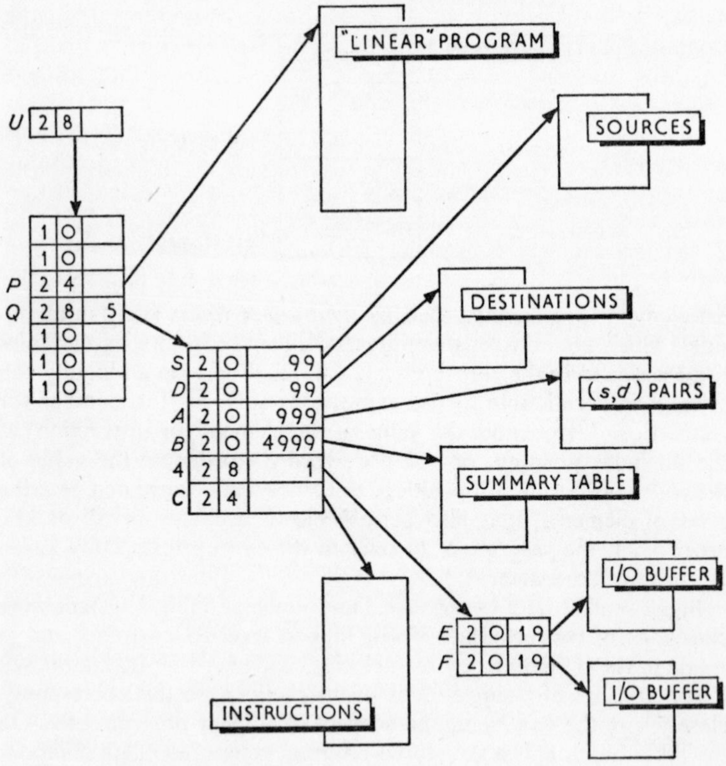

The three levels at which some subdivision of the store is desirable are illustrated by Fig. 2.

    (i) In a multiprogramming machine, to distinguish one program from another, e.g. codewords P and Q.

    (ii) In a single program, to distinguish independent sets of data or instructions, e.g. *A,B,C*, etc. The sets at this level are commonly referred to as 'program segments'.

(iii) In a single segment, to allow for the description of data or instructions which fall naturally into a hierarchical pattern, e.g. *E,F*.

We now examine the conditions under which separability can be maintained. The information in a (tag 2) codeword is sufficient to derive the address (and hence the value) of any element in the set it defines. From the address of *U*, for example, it is possible to access any element in the store. On the other hand, it is *not* possible to derive the codeword *S* from the address of an element in the set *S*, i.e. to traverse the diagram against the direction of the arrows. Hence, from the address of the codeword *P*, only elements in the program *P* can be accessed, and similarly for *Q*. It follows that full separation of programs is achieved if access is allowed only to their own program codewords, and to no higher structural level. Temporary isolation of a substructure, such as required for autonomous data transfers, is obtained by marking (tag 1) the codeword defining the substructure. In this way, any attempt to access it leads to an escape action, which can prevent the access from succeeding until the mark is removed. Referring again to Fig. 2, the codewords *E* and *F* can be alternately 'locked out' in this way while data transfers take place.

The mechanisation of the tree addressing system is reflected in the way programs are written. Given a symbol '*S*' denoting the address of a codeword, it is possible to specify a sequence of index values, $i_1, i_2, \ldots, i_k$, which can be used to select an element at the kth level of the store below *S*, if it exists. In the Basic Language, such a selection is indicated by an expression of the form '$S.i_1.i_2. \ldots .i_k$', which is known as a *compound name based on S*. Provided the base selections are made *at or below* the level of the program codeword, there is no possibility of a programmer referring to elements outside his own store, although we shall see that there are certain situations in which such references may be allowed.

The character of a computer system depends very strongly on the permitted form of compound names: how the bases and indices are specified, how the 'dot' operation is mechanised, how long a path is permitted, and what auxiliary information is made available en route. These decisions in turn affect the way the store is controlled, and the degree of flexibility permitted to the programmer. Most contemporary machines offer only a very stunted tree, but a number of attempts have been made to develop more general systems, and they will be discussed in the present chapter after a brief survey of the alternative possibility, of consolidating entire programs into single blocks of storage.

19

2.1 Storage mapping functions

Those structural characteristics of a problem which are not matched by the computer system on which it is solved must be accounted for in the logic of the instructions it obeys. In Chapter 1, we referred to the process of 'absorbing' the structure into the program. More precisely this means providing a formula for each part of the *conceptual* store structure, thus relating it to a position in the computer's store. It is of interest to examine the implications of absorbing a tree structure into a linear store. Using compound names for elements of the tree, we seek a function $Loc(\eta)$, where η is a compound name, whose value is a position in the linear store, i.e. the location number of the element denoted by η.

For a given tree, there are many ways of taking its terminal elements and fitting them as blocks of words in the linear store. Scanning the tree in an orderly fashion, the position of any set is determined by summing the store requirements of sets in preceding branches. If the tree has any local regularity, the summation may be abbreviated by using a formula, as was done in the example used in Chapter 1 (p. 5), or in the notation of the present chapter (letting 'y' denote the matrix of results):

$$Loc \; ('y.\,s.\,d') = f + 5*s*Length \; (y.0) + 5*d \qquad (2.1.1)$$

where f depends on the store required for preceding sets.

More generally, any regular k-dimensional array S leads to a relation of the form:

$$Loc \; ('S.i_1.i_2. \quad \ldots \quad .i_k') = a_0 + a_1*i_1 + a_2*i_2 + \ldots + a_k*i_k \qquad (2.1.2)$$

where a_0 depends on the preceding elements of the tree, and $a_1, a_2, \ldots, a_k$ are derived from the lengths in each dimension.

Relations such as (2) and (3) are commonly referred to as 'storage mapping functions' (SMF's). It is the task of a linearising assembler or translator to derive SMF's according to the rules of the source language, and to insert orders to evaluate them when required. An optimising translator may go to considerable lengths to derive difference relations from (2.1.2) in order to step from one store position to another without recomputing the entire SMF. Also if the values of some of the a_j and i_j ($j = 1, \ldots, k$) are known at translation time, the calculation would be carried out in part by the translator.

In general, a SMF reduces to a constant term a and a variable b. In a conventional machine, the variable part is calculated when required and stored in a modifier register X. To access the required data it is then sufficient to use an instruction with an address field containing a, and the modifier code for X. If a difference relation is being used to calculate the SMF, the address field may be zero, or

20

a small integer; if there is no variable part, the modifier will then be zero and access to the data is direct, *provided* the address field is large enough for *a*. The exact size of *a* is not usually known at translation time, and the fact that instructions must be assembled to allow for the worst case can lead to inefficiency. Indirect addressing mechanisms may be used in conjunction with various modification rules to improve the efficiency of translation, but it should be noted that they add nothing to the characterisation of the store structure as a single sequence of equal sized elements.

The cost of the above instructions, which is the cost of absorbing structure, varies from one machine or application to the next. Provided the address field is always large enough for *a*, there is no strong bias in favour of any particular instruction pattern, but if the address field is relatively small it becomes important to derive difference relationships in order to achieve efficient code. What is most important, however, is that such absorption techniques are only applicable to *fixed*, *regular* data structures of uniform size, for which the 'preceding' tree elements occupy a fixed amount of core space, in situations where the selected operand is a *single* data element.

Moreover, the SMF as expressed by (2·1·2) is valid only as long as the indices satisfy relations of the form:

$$\left.\begin{array}{l} 0 \leqslant i_1 < Length\ (S) \\ 0 \leqslant i_2 < Length\ (S.i_1) \\ \quad \cdots \\ 0 \leqslant i_k < Length\ (S.i_1.i_2.\ \ \ldots\ \ .i_{k-1}) \end{array}\right\} \qquad (2\cdot1\cdot3)$$

The evaluation of (2·1·2) should therefore be accompanied by a check that (2·1·3) is satisfied: in practice this would add so much to the computation time that it is normally left to the programmer to apply overall checks as appropriate. The consequent programming and debugging costs are not known, but are almost certainly high.

It might be inferred that nothing can be said for using SMF's, and that they should be forgotten in future. To do so would be just as unwise as adhering to the von Neumann machine. For there are many problems using (at least locally) fixed structures, whose indices are constant or can be proved to lie within range, for which the SMF's reduce almost to vanishing point and represent the best solution to the problem. The techniques for mapping into a single linear store apply equally to individual data sets, the SMF's being used to provide index values rather than location numbers. Quite apart from problems which naturally fall into this category, the inheritance of SMF's has been pressed into service in the definition of structure in some conventional languages[5] and must therefore be perpetuated. Finally, it will be seen that SMF's are not confined to representing tree structures, and are used extensively in the handling of complex local data relationships; so in spite of their disadvantages in the large, they will continue to find representation in order codes.

2.2 The Rice University computer

In the years prior to 1958, at least two important principles of programming emerged. The first was the use of segmented programs as a development technique, enabling parts of a program to be corrected and recompiled without having to reprocess the entire program. The effective mechanism for doing this was the *loading* or *consolidating* program which computed the a's required by SMF's, and stored them in instructions immediately prior to execution. The second principle was embodied in list processing languages[6]: that store structure should be seen as a concept independent of instructions and data, deserving a general and abstract formulation. It was natural to apply the second principle to the first[4], and the results obtained from doing so have had considerable influence on the form of the Basic Machine.

The Rice computer is not a multiprogramming machine, so that the introduction of tree storage is motivated by the need to represent structure at segment level and below. The codeword contains, beside the information already described:

the 'external' *index value c* used by the programmer to refer to the first element of the set; and
a *modifier* address X;

The position of the set in core is indicated by storing in the codeword the location number of the first element, b, decremented by c.

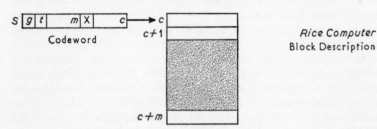

Rice Computer
Block Description

The basic *dot operation* of stepping from codeword S to the address of the ith element of the set it defines is carried out as follows: first the index value i is loaded into the modifier selected by X; then the codeword S is accessed; the result is the location number $b - c + i$. (Thus an index value c results in the location b of the first stored element.) However, if the type t indicates that the subset consists of codewords, the addressing operation is automatically carried forward another step; in general, the next level of

22

codewords will select another modifier, which must also have been preloaded. The action continues until type t indicates that a data or instruction set has been reached. The index value is not checked to ensure that it lies in the range:

$$c \leqslant i \leqslant c + m$$

so that the mechanism of the 'dot' operation is not exact, although an escape tag g can be set to cause interpretive comparison.

The Rice mechanism has the disadvantage of preassigning the modifiers to be used at each structural level. In a general programming system, one can only use a simple assignment rule, so that clashes are almost inevitable. There is also some disadvantage in specifying the index value i before the codeword address S; in practice it is more common to hold S constant while i varies than vice versa.

Once the description of sets has been formalised, it becomes possible to incorporate operations on sets as part of the computer's 'function code'. The basic structural operations provided through the computer's store control system allow for the *creation* and *deletion* of sets, and the *insertion* (or removal) of elements. Input, output, and arithmetical operations on vectors and matrices follow directly[7], and the language used to operate the machine makes extensive use of the tree structure. In the Rice computer, all such operations are carried out interpretively, but it is clear that once the engineering model recognises 'non-scalar' entities they should be admitted as arguments of machine instructions. Whether the instructions are carried out directly 'by hardware' or not is outside the scope of the model.

The storage tree is based on two sets of codewords called the 'system base' and the 'program base'. The former defines permanent system tables and routines, many of which are available for use by the programmer. The latter defines the data and instructions of the (single) program currently being obeyed. The base elements are identified symbolically by the programmer, two tables being maintained to relate symbols to the base indices. The system base occupies a fixed position in the store, and can therefore be addressed by using a location number rather than a 'principal codeword'. The program base is an element of the system base, index 82 (see Fig. 3). Therefore a compound name of the form:

$$S.i_1.i_2 \tag{2·2·1}$$

would be assembled into instructions evaluating:

$$i_0.i_1.i_2 \tag{2·2·2}$$

if S has index i_0 in the system base or:

$$82.i_0.i_1.i_2 \tag{2·2·3}$$

23

if S is in the program base. However, we have to make allowance for the fact that in any segmented system, the value of i_0 may not be known (if S is in the program base) when the compound name based on 'S' is translated. It is therefore convenient to direct all references to the program base from an instruction segment through a 'connection table' at the end of the segment, containing one entry for each element referred to (see Fig. 3). The connection table is completed when the segment is loaded. The entry for S consists of the symbolic name 'S' and an address equivalent to '$82.i_0$', so the path length starting from the instruction is the same as in (2·2·2).

Fig. 3. Communication by connection table

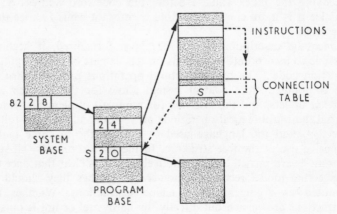

The primary disadvantage of the tree structure can be observed to be the number of separate steps required to obtain an element of information, and the remedy of deriving bases at the lowest levels of the structure suggests itself. In the Rice computer, this simply means allowing the programmer to compute the location number of an element and modify it by adding or subtracting small integers to address adjacent elements. The control register works in a similar way: control jumps and data accesses *within* a segment are computed relative to the control register, and program segments are not dependent on their position in store. Repetitive operations on sets are thus programmed by conventional methods. By such means the percentage of store accesses caused by stepping through the storage tree has been reduced to 5%–10%. The price to be paid is that the store structure becomes partially *location number dependent* at certain times, and the consequent restrictions on the definition of sets, storage of links and use of parameters feed back in one form or another to the programming languages in use on the machine. While the sum total of restrictions falls far short of those in a conventional storage system, they lack the simplicity of the 'Thou shalt not . . .' variety, and it is important to eliminate them.

One other important lesson can be drawn from the Rice machine. The system requires that codewords should not be stored within instruction sets, since it is not economical to maintain them there. Therefore, any quantity with explicit structure must be treated as 'external' to the instruction sequence, even though it may be logically 'internal' or localised in use. It is bad in principle to establish an artificial relation between two independent concepts, and practice confirms it in this instance. To provide structural information within a segment is important not only in achieving uniformity of programming ideas, but also in raising system efficiency by reducing store fragmentation; the *relative* codeword system introduced in the Basic Machine will be seen to serve this purpose.

Several implementations of a tree-structured store in a single-program environment have been reported in recent years, amongst them EULER[8], the Integrated Civil Engineering System[9], the SPAN system [10], and JOSS[11], the last named illustrating particularly well the use of on-line structural control. All the implementations are based on conventional machines, so their efficiency, measured by execution speeds, tends to be low. They are of interest from the point of view of programming language features for the control of compound names, escape actions, type discrimination, and operations on arrays. Unlike list processing systems, the cost of maintaining a dynamic tree storage structure is small, for three main reasons:

(i) the number of independent storage blocks is relatively small;

(ii) the only cross-references which need maintaining are the codewords themselves (provided the program base is held stationary, the connection tables need not be altered); and

(iii) when conventional store mapping methods are applicable, the tree structure allows them to be used. Hence it might be argued that tree maintenance costs are not entirely 'overheads', because the programmer can choose to use a tree only when he gains something from it.

2.3 The Burroughs B5000

The first commercial computer system to make use of a tree structure was the Burroughs B5000, also remembered as one of the earliest to incorporate a push-down stack for operands[3]. The machine is probably unique in being programmed almost exclusively in high-level languages (variants of Algol, Cobol and Fortran). We shall consider the consequence of this in the system design, but more immediately relevant is the fact that detailed information about the machine language programming techniques is not readily

25

available. In the following brief description some simplifications are made in order to concentrate on structural aspects of the machine, and the terminology already introduced in connection with the Rice computer is used.

The motivation for the tree structure is to separate programs in a multiprogramming environment, and to distinguish segments within a program, allowing particularly for automatic lock-out during peripheral transfers, and for automatic integration of the core and drum system into a 'single level store'. Comparatively little attention is paid to segment substructure. The system store can be regarded as a set of codewords, each defining a program base, but the elements in any base are a *mixture* of numerical data and codewords, the distinction being made by holding one of the tag bits in *each* word. The codewords contain, beside the usual information, the starting location d of each set on drum storage.

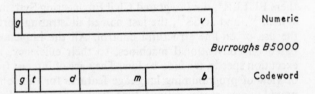

In a stack machine, operands brought to the top of the stack automatically 'push down' any which are already there. All arithmetic operations are performed on the top two elements, which are designated the A and B registers on the B5000, A being on top of B. The instructions are either functions of the implied operands A and B or commands for loading A with either:

(a) an integer; or
(b) an address of an element of the program base; or
(c) the value of an element of the program base.

However, if in (b) or (c) the base element is a codeword S, and B contains a number i then the result of the instruction is either:

(b′) the address of $S.i$; or
(c′) the value of $S.i$.

Further element selection, such as '$S.i_1.i_2$' would require, is not easily achieved.

The basic 'dot' operation involves checking the base element S to see that it is a codeword, that the set it refers to is in core and not locked out, and checking that the index i is positive and not greater than the limit m. If the set is held on drum and not in core, space must be found allowing it to be transferred to core, then the instruction is repeated; if the set is locked out, the instruction is suspended until the data transfer is completed successfully; if the index value is not within range, a store violation is reported. The hardware interpretation of g and m is thus sufficiently thorough to ensure the segment protection and lock-out, and integration of drum and core storage, required in the system design.

It can be seen that it is possible to form an address of an array element, such as $S.i$, submerging it in the stack, then to initiate a peripheral transfer involving S, with the address still in the stack and not locked out. To guard against the possibility of inconsistent results, it would be sufficient to scan the stack looking for addresses referring to the set S and setting their tags to cause escape actions. However, there may be prior reasons for knowing that no such references exist: if the program is generated by a higher-level language, then the discipline of stack use is often such as not to leave addresses in it when issuing an input or output command—the address $S.i$ is recomputed from the codeword when needed; and in many instances the data have to be edited, blocked, or otherwise manipulated by trusted system routines before being transferred, in which cases the areas involved in transfers will not be accessible to the user's program. In general, therefore, it is not justifiable to scan the stack to lock out addresses, unless the programmer asks for it to be done, as he might do when developing part of a program.

More serious problems arise in connection with any change of structure or physical reorganisation which may require the store control routines to find all addresses pointing into a set S and to update them. For these reasons, the ability to scan the program stack and to detect addresses pointing into a given area of store emerges as an important requirement in store management. Just how important depends on other factors, to be discussed in Chapter 5, but in connection with the B5000 it is again possible to see that the use of conventional high-level languages can lead to a simplification of demands for storage. In Cobol and Fortran, for example, sets (i.e. arrays and subroutines) are never redefined and not deleted until a program terminates, at which time the stack is also deleted.

Tagged storage

Introduction of a set of independently tagged elements closed the logical gap which the Rice University system required programmers to fill. Whether it should be addressed as a stack, as on the Burroughs machine, or in a more general way, is an independent and somewhat secondary issue. Its effect is to allow the formation of sequences of elements of different types. This is important to the input language, in which such items often arise as lists of 'parameters'. It is also important to the machine design, since it enables the instruction code to benefit from the use of a group of general-purpose central registers without sacrificing the protective features of the type

27

interpretation rules. It will be shown in Chapter 3 how the tags which have been associated with codewords extend to meet this more general requirement.

Address calculations

Although the temporary storage required for numerical results can be provided by data sets (type 0), this is not so for addresses, since the only stored addressing material (type 8) is constrained in codewords designed to preserve the tree structure. The ability to overwrite codewords with addresses or numerical information would significantly increase the cost of store maintenance. (In the B5000, it can be seen that it is not a simple matter to form the address of a *codeword* in the program base.) Hence the fully tagged store is the only region where intermediate addresses can be held. As an example of the importance of this facility, refer again to Fig. 2 and consider the calculation of addresses in the buffer E, which have the compound name '$U.Q.4.0.i$', based on U. We can assume the first two steps, giving '$U.Q.4$', to be taken by the base selection order through the mechanism of the connection table. There remain two more dot operations to select an element of E; clearly the process of scanning becomes inefficient if the entire compound name has to be re-evaluated for each value of i. On the other hand, if the constant part '$U.Q.4.0$' can be calculated and held as an address in a register X, then the repeated evaluation consists simply of '$X.i$'; better still, if '$U.Q.4.0.0$' can be evaluated as the address of the *first* element of E, together with the *limit value*, then scanning the buffer is achieved by successive modifications of the address, and is comparable in efficiency with conventional methods.

The above techniques are fully developed in the Basic Machine, which has a set of explicitly addressable registers. In the B5000, the stack mechanism does not lend itself to the manipulation of intermediate results, and greater reliance is placed on recomputing addresses, and restricting the useful depth of the storage tree, so that address paths are short.

Store sharing

The concurrent execution of two or more programs raises the question of whether they might share the same subroutines or tables of constants. It is necessary, for any two independent programs to work in this way, that the shared information be invariant, and therefore that the hardware observe a 'read-only' rule for shared sets. This is not possible for data on the B5000, but it is possible for instructions, since any attempt to access an instruction set is treated as a control jump to the first instruction in the set. It is thus possible for two programs P, Q to share a common subroutine S in a third program R as in Fig. 4. The purpose of this is purely to economise in storage space; it is logically equivalent to having two copies of S, one for P and the other for Q. A common situation is that R is a 'housekeeping' program which may be used by several programs at once without waste of space.

Fig. 4. A shared subroutine S

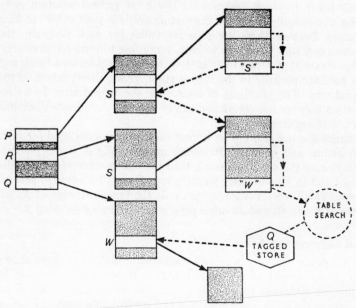

The use of shared information has several general consequences for any addressing system. Clearly, the consolidation process outlined in Section 2.1 cannot be applied simultaneously to three programs such as P, Q and R, to include just one copy of S. Store sharing implies that addresses do not have the simple arithmetic properties assumed in the von Neumann model. The codeword system recognises separate store areas in a satisfactory way, and provides the means of controlling address calculation, but the method of cross-referencing embodied in the connection table cannot, in general, be applied to a routine such as S. Consider the situation when S makes use of a set of working variables which it refers to as 'W'. Since S is invariant, W must be external to S and contained in the program base of *each* program using S. Thus P, Q and R each have their versions of W, and the method of cross-referencing must select the one appropriate to the program using S at a given instant, e.g. by implicitly selecting an element in the current program base.

However, the mechanism cannot be left as it stands, because it requires entries to be set aside in every program base for W, and all other entities defined for use by shared routines. Whilst such assignments may be made in the limited context of a group of heavily used system routines, it would not be possible to cater for all the requirements of a growing system in this way because the bases would become intolerably large and unmanageable, though the problem is less severe on a machine allowing multi-level structures with fewer top-level codewords. The most general solution is to refer dynamically to a table connecting symbols such as 'W' to base indices. Because there are separate tables for each program, the indices can vary from base to base, according to local requirements. This means that access to W is slow, but once made, its address can be held temporarily in the tagged store, giving direct access in the usual way. The problems of addressing the tagged store in an invariant way are less severe and can be solved by moderate discipline in use of registers.

Store sharing also has an impact on the techniques used for store allocation and recovery. Referring again to Fig. 4, if the physical location of the set S is altered, then the datum address in its codeword and in all addresses pointing into S must be adjusted accordingly. This involves scanning not only the tagged storage of R, but also of P and Q, and all other programs which may be using S.

2.4 Segmenting schemes

The main difficulty in using a tree-structured store has been shown to be the length of compound names. It has been overcome by allowing addresses to be constructed and retained to obtain direct access to the store. Since addresses and control links contain location numbers, they must be tagged and stored in such a way that they can readily be updated in the event of a change in the structure or physical disposition of the tree.

An alternative solution is to restrict the depth of tree, e.g. by ignoring subsegment structure, and to carry compound names in indicial form throughout the program. Each compound name $S.i_1$ reduces to a base index i_0 for S and segment index i_1 which may be stored as a binary 'address' with the value $2^q i_0 + i_1$, where 2^q is the maximum length of any single segment. If 2^p segments are allowed for, then all addresses are $p + q$ bits long, in practice about 30 bits.

p	q	
i_0	i_1	Segment Element Address

The addressing mechanism is such that on each store reference i_0 is used to obtain the segment codeword, which is then modified by i_1 to access the store. The intermediate address is never retained for subsequent use, and consequently tagged storage is not strictly

30

necessary. The resulting mechanism typifies the 'segmenting' approach to store organisation which has been used in a number of current machine designs[12, 13]. It differs from a codeword system in its logical and practical consequences.

As noted already, the storage tree has only one level below the program base, i.e. all subsegment structure must be absorbed into coded instructions. Temporary structural isolation is afforded by tag 1 (escape) codewords in the usual way, and this protection is complete, since the codeword stands on the only route into the segment. Hence there is nothing to correspond to a tagged store and the programming rules associated with it. Two important corollaries follow:

First, in the central registers of the machine there is no possibility of making an automatic distinction between addresses and data, nor indeed between different numeric representations. Such discriminations must be made by the function code itself, in the conventional way.

Second, although the physical distribution of segments may be changed freely to meet system requirements, the variations in conceptual structure are restricted to attachment or removal of elements at one end only; it is not possible to insert or remove elements at the beginning (i.e. before the first element) or within the set. In order to do that it would be necessary to update all relevant existing addresses, and that possibility has been excluded.

The method of inter-segment communication carries over directly from the codeword system. For nonsharable segments, the connection table contains indices of the current program base. For shared segments, a number of indices may be given fixed significance for every program (in the ICT Atlas, over half of the segment numbers are reserved for privileged system use). In general, however, a symbolic reference must be made initially. This is converted to an index in the current program base by a table search, and that index is retained for immediate use. A practicable arrangement would be to assign two segment indices (say 1 and 2) for the symbol table and index store in each program. The latter is controlled as a stack by the routine entry and exit mechanisms so that, once having stored a cross-reference index when calling a routine into use, it may subsequently be retrieved relative to a stack pointer, itself an address of the form '2.j' held in a modifier register.

The most obvious practical effect of a segmented address mechanism is that every store access refers to the program base before obtaining a stored unit of data or instruction. The nominal amount of activity required from the primary store is thereby doubled; if a fixed length paging mechanism is superposed on the segment structure, the nominal factor may increase to three or four, and indirect addressing such as required by the connection table could double

31

this figure. Proposals for mitigating the scheme's effects on system performance are now abundant in computer literature, and one scheme has been in satisfactory operation on the ICT Atlas computer for a number of years[13]. Little is known at present of the effectiveness of some of the more elaborate systems designed for multi-access use, and particularly for store sharing. It is inevitable, however, that a logical network interposed between processor and main store will delay store accesses by a small amount no matter how effective it is. Although the overall time delay might be concealed by other circumstances, the effort of recovering to near normal execution speeds absorbs an appreciable amount of logical power which could well be used elsewhere.

3

BASIC MACHINE

In this chapter the central registers, the instructions, and the sequencing rule of a Basic Machine are discussed. In the engineering model defined by Basic Language, parts of the machine will remain hidden from the user in the interest of security, speed or generality. The same interests must be served in von Neumann models by designating registers, store areas and functions which may only be used in a privileged control state, but the advent of address and instruction protection will be seen to permit more sophisticated concealment tactics to be used in Basic Language. For the present, we need consider only the behaviour of a single central processing unit in a Basic Machine system, assuming the other system components to be conventionally specified.

The tree structure was proposed in the first place to separate one program from another, and to distinguish separate segments within a program. In practice, the 'program codewords' are quite unimportant, and it is not essential to provide for their direct recognition by hardware, since the construction and use of the program base enable it to be accessed by addressing through a connection table. It is also seen in practice that the initial concept of a tree is qualified by the existence of computed addresses, providing direct paths into data, instruction and codeword sets. Separation is then achieved by monitoring addresses and by appealing to the properties of the machine programming language, and thereby to the instructions representing it. Both addresses and instructions must be distinguishable as stored information, since only then can the representation of programs be relied upon. We are thus led to devise some formal way of identifying instructions and addresses, and to require that the hardware act accordingly. It happens that exactly the same mechanism is necessary to admit dynamic interpretation of operand types, and to insulate the majority of programmers from local optimisations of the address and instruction codes, so the conventions which follow achieve three of the general objectives of the engineering model. As is frequently the case in the design of logical systems, once a component has been included for one or two major reasons, the design changes to exploit it fully. The subsections which follow are concentrated on the less common features of a Basic Machine

33

processor; in many respects, not discussed, the choice before the machine designer is essentially the same as on a conventional machine; in particular, no reference is made to the function of the central processor in controlling peripheral data channels.

To illustrate the coding in detail, information units of a *byte* (8 bits), *word* (32 bits) and *double word* (64 bits) are used. The advantages of using exact divisions of multiples of a word size are obvious, but the use of a particular word length is not critical to the system; the predominant data widths would in practice determine the word size. It is assumed that all sets of similar elements are packed efficiently and retrieved without concern by the programmer for word boundaries or any other physical storage parameters.

3.1 Tag and type codes

The labels used in the Basic Machine are of two sorts: a *tag* code for individual elements; and a *type* code for sets of similar elements. The advantage of using types is that they represent a very small overhead in the quantity of information stored, and in practice the bulk of information can be arranged as sets of similar elements. The important situations where the label may vary from one element of a set to the next are handled by allowing each to carry a tag; the set they compose is then said to be of 'mixed' type. The amount of storage required for any element is called its *size*, which is a function of the type. A set of mixed type must allow the possibility of any element assuming the maximum size (in the present case, 64 bits including the tag).

A choice of tag codes for the Basic Machine is given in Table 1 (allowing for possible extensions, a 3-bit tag is assumed in data formats). Tag 0 labels the binary data word, which takes part in elementary arithmetical and logical operations. As an arithmetic

quantity, it is treated as an integer, with two's complement representation. The tag is not part of the integer. The shaded portion of the register is unused (see diagram).

Tag 1 is used to label any element which cannot be directly recognised by hardware, such as an out-of-range numerical result or an undefined item. When presented as an argument of a machine function, a tag 1 element normally causes a trap to an escape routine. Up to 32 information bits plus a type code are associated with it, for interpretation by the escape routine which may permit the calculation to continue or cause a control jump to a prescribed part of the program. (The escape type codes are given in Table 6.)

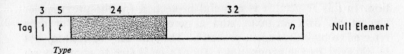

Tag

3 5   24   32

| 1 | t | | n | Null Element

Type

Tag 2 labels an address of a *sequence* of m elements of given type, starting at location b (the first byte of the first element). An address has the following format:

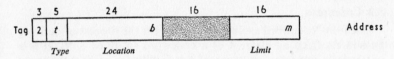

Tag

3 5   24   16   16

| 2 | t | b | | m | Address

Type   Location   Limit

If m is zero, the address is said to be *singular*, since it points to a sequence of only one element (at b). The maximum length of any addressable sequence is 65 536 elements, of any size. The type codes (t) are given in Table 2, and discussed below. (The address format allows for extension to 32 distinct type codes.)

The numeric element (tag 3) admits the representation of a larger class of numbers than tag 0. It is assumed that the integers are included in the numeric class which follows a conventional 'floating point' practice. Its exact format is unimportant in the present context, but it is proposed that up to 61 bits are available for arithmetic purposes.

It will be noted that there is no tag code corresponding to an 'instruction': it is not possible (or meaningful) to extract an instruction from a code sequence and operate on it in any way. The assembly program constructs code as sets of binary words, and after they are fully checked it changes the type description to 'instruction' by special dispensation of the store control routines.

The type codes of Table 2 should be compared with the tags in Table 1. In general, when an element is retrieved from storage, the type code in its address determines the consequent tag (this is not true for types 10 and 11, where the element carries its own tag). The store access mechanism operates on an address and combines the formation of the tag with the reconstruction of the element itself; it is not essential for the element to be stored in precisely the form it assumes when tagged. For example, sets of type 0, 1, 2 or 3 all give rise to tag 0 elements, the bytes (type 1, 3) being expanded to 32 bits by extension of the sign digit, except in logical functions, in which a 'zero' extension field is used. Similarly, numeric elements may be stored in long or short form, the latter representing a subset of the tag 3 elements, which can be used to halve the amount of storage space required by sets of low-precision data.

With integer, numeric and mixed sets, the type code distinguishes a 'read-only' status, intended as a protection for constant informa-

35

tion. In this respect, it is a useful protection for the programmer against his own mistakes, and a necessary protection for data referred to by independent processes. The read-only status may not be changed by the programmer, though he is free to copy any set and use it as he likes. Instruction sets have execute-only status by definition of machine functions; the type code is used to distinguish different modes of execution, which are under the control of the programmer.

3.2 Codewords

The term 'codeword evaluation' is used for the process of deriving an address from an element of a codeword set (type 8, 9). It is a particularly important instance of the facility for reconstituting an element before processing it. The definition of machine functions makes it impossible to store an address back into a codeword set, which can therefore be regarded as having read-only status.

A codeword normally contains the same information as an address referring to a sequence of stored elements of specified type. The term 'set' is used for the sequence defined by a codeword; the derived address refers to the same sequence, but the machine addressing functions permit *sub*sequences of the original one to be addressed. It follows that the sequence defined by an address is always a set, or part of a set, and never overlaps a set boundary, and on this fact the store protection system is based. If a codeword does not refer explicitly to a set, its tag code is 1, and codeword evaluation leads to programmed interpretation. In all other instances, the codeword has tag 2.

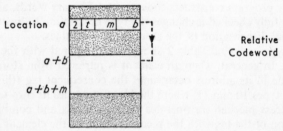

The location number (b) contained in a codeword is either a direct reference to store or a byte count relative to the location of the codeword itself. The alternatives are termed *absolute* (type 8) and *relative* (type 9) codewords respectively, the defined elements of any codeword set being all of the same form. It is convenient to depic at relative codeword set by including it in the same 'block' as the information to which it refers, since the store allocation routines will ignore all substructure, treating the block as a single entity. Relative codewords are formed by the Basic Language assembly

36

program in the course of constructing blocks; it is so arranged that blocks cannot include type 8, 10 or 11 elements, and that all relative addresses refer within the same block. In relative codewords, *m* and *b* are restricted to 12 bits each in order to pack them into a single word. Relative sets are thus restricted to 4096 elements, and to start within 4096 bytes after their defining codeword. Absolute sets have the same range as addresses.

Notation for tags

The action of machine functions is strongly dependent on tags, and it is convenient to introduce a special notation for describing various tag and type combinations. In general, an element with tag 2, type *t*, is said to have 'tag 2(*t*)', equally for addresses and codewords. Thus the address of a byte sequence has tag 2(1), or 2(3) if read-only. Certain combinations of type categories are assumed by the following extensions of the description of tag 2 elements:

'tag 2(N)' referring to an integer or numeric sequence, i.e. type 0, 1, 2, 3, 12, 13, 14 or 15;

'tag 2(I)' referring to an instruction sequence, i.e. type 4, 5, 6 or 7;

'tag 2(M)' referring to a mixed sequence i.e. type 10, 11;

'tag 2(C)' referring to a codeword sequence, i.e. type 8, 9.

An escape codeword or register of type *t* is similarly described as having 'tag 1(*t*)'. Thus a file address has tag 1(7), and functions which operate on files would normally require one or more arguments of this sort.

3.3 Register assignment

The Basic Machine provides for sixteen elements directly selected by the instruction code. They are referred to as the registers '*X0*', '*X1*', ..., '*X9*', '*XA*', ..., '*XF*', and the last four have special purposes in the machine specification. In general, a register may be used as a temporary store for any tagged element, so that the size of each register is 64 bits, and the formats it can assume are as described in Section 3.1. The registers are equivalent, as a group of stores, to a sequence of elements of mixed type. No other directly addressable elements are required to implement Basic Language. As will be seen in Chapter 5, this particular number is more than sufficient.

The special purpose registers are as follows:

Control number XC

XC contains the address of the instruction currently being obeyed, and therefore has tag 2(I). The limit value normally found in an address has no sensible meaning in a control sequence and is omitted from *XC*. The type code I selects the control *mode*, and two further bits *c* are used as testable *condition indicators* which are set by certain machine functions:

	3	5	24	30	2	
Tag	2	1	*b*		*c*	Control Number

The content of *XC* is changed by control jumps: in relative jumps the increment is computed and checked by the assembly program, and no limit comparison is required; absolute jumps are made via addresses or codewords of tag 2(I), the tag being examined by the jump function to ensure its validity. Relative jumps leave I and *c* unchanged; absolute jumps through a codeword reset *c* to zero and reset I according to the type value in the destination codeword.

XC may be placed also as a link address in another register, or in the program store. Special machine functions are provided for returning control to a link address; although it is possible in machine code to reset *XC* by copying information directly into it, Basic Language does not reflect the presence of the control number as a central register.

Process base register XD

The idea of a distinct program base for each separate activity, which characterises the systems described in Chapter 2, is not perpetuated in the Basic Machine. In its place, a form of tagged store known as the 'process base' is defined for each independent control sequence. The address of the process base is held in *XD*, which has tag 2(10).

Three separate regions are distinguished in the process base:

(a) *Register store*. The first sixteen elements of the sequence *XD* are identified with the central registers.

(b) *Extended register store*. The elements indexed from 16 upwards may be used to hold copies of register values. The extended register store is addressed symbolically in Basic Language, index values being assigned by the translator. The length of the sequence is predetermined for each activity when it is initiated, and normally comprises about fifty words.

(c) *Register stack*. Following the e.r.s. is a sequence of variable length, controlled as a stack. The limit value of *XD* determines the current extent of the stack. Special functions are provided for transferring elements between the top of the stack and the central registers.

It can be seen that *XD* really supplies two addressing bases—one for the registers and extended register store, and one for the top of the stack. The physical limit of the base is marked by a special stack element.

38

Escape registers XE, XF

To fulfill the requirement for fast escape actions described in Chapter 1, two central registers are reserved for communication with interpretive routines. Details of their use depend strongly on the machine hardware, which is outside the scope of the engineering model. Nonprivileged Basic Language programs do not have direct access to *XE* and *XF*, and user-defined escape actions must be expressed as operations on the registers *X0–X9*, or as indirect operations on *XE* and *XF*, using special expressions recognised by the translator. The escape registers may also be used to give rapid response to certain classes of external events serviced by users' routines (including the changes of state in peripheral devices).

3.4 Fetch and store conventions

Machine functions operate on stored information through the use of addresses held in registers. Because an address generally defines more than one item of information, the convention is adopted of operating on only the *first* element of a sequence, unless stated otherwise in the function definition. A unique numerical operand can therefore be represented by a register with tag 0 or 3, in which cases the register contains the operand, or with tag 2(N), when it contains the address. In all arithmetic and addressing functions, when a numerical value is required it is automatically obtained from a tag 2(N) argument by fetching the first addressed element, with tag 0 or 3 as appropriate. Such interpretation of the argument is referred to as the 'AutoFetch', or 'A/F' convention. It does not apply to tag 2(C) or 2(I) arguments. In the case of tag 2(M), the first addressed element is obtained with its tag, then the A/F convention is applied to that, recycling if necessary.

Most arithmetic and logical functions have two arguments, and produce a result which overwrites the first one of them. If that had been evaluated by the A/F convention, the result must be stored as the first of a sequence of given type, and must therefore be expressible within the same type convention. In general a tag 3 result is converted to integer form before storing in a type 0 or 1 sequence, and a tag 0 result is converted to tag 3 before storing in a tag 12 or 13 sequence. For types 1 and 13, some truncation is necessary; in the former, the most significant digits are lost after arithmetic functions, and an invalid result signal is given if they are non-zero. Attempts to store to sequences of type 2, 3, 14 or 15 fail because of their read-only status. The above rules are applied automatically when the first argument of an arithmetic function has tag 2(N). They are briefly referred to as the 'AutoStore', or 'A/S' convention. They do not apply to 2(C) or 2(I) arguments. Special functions are provided for copying register values into sets of mixed type.

3.5 Sequencing conventions

After completing an instruction, the control register XC is normally incremented by the correct number of bytes to obtain the next in sequence. Transfers of control within a sequence are effected by adding a (signed) relative location number to XC. The assembly program checks that no storage violations can occur as a result of normal sequencing or control jumps. Relative jumps may be made dependent on the condition indicators c (held in XC), or on the value of a single register.

Unconditional jumps may be made to any tag 2(I) element, acting as a control link: note that a link cannot be modified, since the size of instructions is unknown to the programmer, and special provision is made in the assembly program for constructing relative codeword sets to form what are usually known as 'switch vectors'. A convention similar to AutoFetch is applied to jump functions, in which the destination may be specified by the *address* of a tag 2(I) element.

Marked links

Provision is made for storing a control link in the register stack with an integer mark a in the range 0 to 7.

	3	5	24		3	2	
Tag	2	I	b		a	c	Link (in stack)

The machine function *RET* (return) scans the stack from the top, searching for a link with a mark greater than or equal to a specified value, reducing the limit in XD as it does so. When the link is found, it is removed from the stack and obeyed. Because the operating system stores a link with mark 7 at the beginning of the stack, the search always succeeds. Any other attempt to read a marked element is monitored.

The purpose of the mark convention is to allow the user to establish a hierarchy of points in the stack to which the control sequence may be synchronised without concern for intermediate results. Typical control points are subroutine exits, restarts and error exits. A link may also be stored in a register and then copied to the stack, in which case its mark is zero.

Escape actions

Whether or not a function can be completed successfully depends on its argument tags, types and values. The reasons for failure may be classified as:

(a) *Tag conflict*. The function is not defined for the tag and type combinations of its arguments. This would be the case, for example,

40

If an arithmetic function were applied to a tag 2(C) register, or if either or both arguments had tag 1.

(b) *Invalid result*. The result is out of range of the machine representation, e.g. an arithmetic overflow condition.

(c) *Fail of A/S*. The truncated value obtained by the AutoStore convention has lost some significant digits, e.g. when storing an integer greater than 127 to a byte position.

On detecting a failure, further action depends on locally applied conventions. Tag conflict invariably causes an escape to a set of user- or system-defined routines, which will interpret the condition and continue the calculation, or take an error exit from the program. Invalid results may be 'represented' by tag 1 elements (cf. Table 6) without interrupting the program, or they too may initiate error action; the choice is made dependent on a control mode preset by the programmer. If a tag 1 results, the programmer may act on it immediately by testing the condition indicators, or later by testing the tag code of the result, thus achieving the benefits of both 'hard' and 'soft' overflow detection.

Modes

There are two mode indicators generally available in the Basic Machine. That already mentioned is the 'invalid result' monitor (IR). The second is a 'Trace' control, which can be tested by machine function (JNT), and used to initiate selective output of intermediate results, register values, and control links, in various styles of interpretation appropriate to the program structure and Basic Language symbolism. Mode indicators and condition codes are stored as part of the control link, and are therefore restored when the link is obeyed. When jumping to a new instruction sequence via a codeword, the mode of the latter is mixed with the current control mode, i.e. if control is in Trace (or IR) mode when obeying a jump through a codeword, it continues in Trace (or IR) mode whatever the value of I in the codeword.

3.6 Choice of machine functions

We now discuss the main factors influencing the list of Basic Machine functions. (The names chosen for them are those of Basic Language, where appropriate, but they are to be understood as standing in unique correspondence with a numerical function encoding.) Fundamentally, a function earns its place in the 'hardware' on the grounds of intensity of use or suitability for the methods assumed to generate instructions, but in practice a very few functions account for almost all a processor's time, and it is more often 'ease of use' which is the determining factor in their selection. The conventions of programming, in our case of Basic Language, are therefore decisive.

An alphabetic list of functions is given in Table 3. They are classified into four groups:

Group A : Arithmetic and logical;
　　　 B : Base manipulation;
　　　 C : Control;
　　　 D : Addressing.

Most functions have two arguments, causing a result to overwrite the operand defined by the first, and possibly setting the condition indicators in *XC*. In expressing machine instructions the Basic Language convention of writing the function name between the first and second arguments is adopted, e.g.

$$X3 \quad ADD \quad X5$$

causes the operands selected by *X3* and *X5* to be added, the result replacing the former.

The arithmetic and logical functions (Group A)

Most functions of this group are self-explanatory to the level of detail which concerns us. The AutoFetch and AutoScore conventions apply to both arguments, and the condition indicators are set by the sign and value of the result. The *ADD* function, for example, may be used to add any two numeric or integer quantities, of any size, and takes the place of 64 'add functions' which would be necessary in a fully absorbed function code, when the possible combinations of long and short operands and addresses are accounted for. If overflow occurs, an invalid result is indicated, possibly causing a control trap as discussed in Section 3.5. (The result of adding two integers can always be represented by a tag 3 operand, and need not cause an invalid result until an attempt is made to store it to an integer sequence.) Tag-dependent store operations are carried out by the *MOVE* function, which carries out any necessary type conversion. The *SIZE* function is provided to test the precision of an integer or numeric argument, before attempting to store it. The logical functions (*AND, NEQ, NOT, OR, SH*) are undefined for tag 3 operands.

The base-manipulation functions (Group B)

Base functions are intended for moving tagged elements from one position to another without the intepretation implicit in the other groups. They are generally applicable to sequences of mixed type, and particularly to the process base itself, addressed by *XD*. Thus *COPY* is used to transfer the content of one register to another, whatever their tags; register fetch *RF* moves the first element of a mixed sequence into a given register; and register stores *RS* stores a register to the first position of a given type 10 sequence. In these cases, the AutoFetch and AutoStore rules are not applied.

42

The register stack is accessed by specifying any group of the 16 registers to be transferred to (*DUMP*) or from (*UNDUMP*) the current 'top' of the stack as indicated by *XD*. Stack overflow and underflow are detected by sensing nonzero marks in the first and last positions of the stack, in addition to which a nonzero mark in *any* position causes monitoring action on *UNDUMP*. The sequence of dumping within an instruction is in ascending register number order, and conversely for undumping; any other ordering must be achieved by generating more than one instruction.

Two special functions (*LPB*, *JPB*) are provided for access to the permanent system base by privileged routines, and for the encoding of executive function calls.

The control functions (Group C)

Conditional jumps are always relative, by an amount computed by the assembly program. The eight mnemonic codes used in Basic Language for conditions are given in Table 4, and these are directly represented in the binary instruction format. A conditional jump may also be made (by using *JL* and *JNL*) on the content of a register (*zero* if tag 0 or 3, *singular* if tag 2), combined with a 'countdown' or 'modification by one' action to enable common counting and scanning loops to be programmed compactly.

Unconditional jumps may be made relative to *XC* (i.e. to a position in the current segment), or to an address stored in a register, which must have tag 2(I) or 2(C). In the latter case, the addressed codeword must have tag 2(I). All these checks are performed at run time, and the jump function fails if they are not satisfied.

Conditional jumps cannot store a link; unconditional jumps may. The link is the address of the immediately following instruction, and it can be stored in a register or at the top of the stack with or without a mark. Thus, an unconditional jump, which is written in the form:

$$X6 \quad JSL \quad X1$$

will jump to the destination given by *X1* and store the link address in *X6*. Also, the instruction:

$$2 \quad JSM \quad -12$$

will jump 12 instructions backwards relative to the current instruction, and store the link with mark 2 at the top of the stack. On the other hand:

$$JUMP \quad X6$$

jumps to the address given by *X6*, without storing a link, as required in a simple return from a subroutine. To return via a marked entry in the stack, one would use, e.g.:

$$RET \quad 2$$

43

which starts at the top of the stack, and searches for the first link with mark 2 or greater, which it obeys. The stack limit in XD is reset to point to the entry before the obeyed link.

The addressing functions (Group D)

The least orthodox function group is D. There are two primary operations on an address: to change it to point to a subsequence of that originally addressed, and to fetch the first element into a register. The first is accomplished by MOD and LIM, which chop off elements from the low- and high-index ends of the sequence respectively. In modification, the modifier value is automatically scaled in accordance with the size of element. The second is provided by $LOAD$, whose effect for various argument tags is summarised as follows:

Tag	Result
0,3	Same as argument value
1	Invalid
2(N)	A/F applies
2(C)	Codeword evaluation applies
2(I)	Invalid
2(M)	A/F applies

The $LOAD$ function therefore combines all the access conventions previously encountered. It is frequently followed by subset selection when applied to tag 2(C); in particular the DOT function results in the singular address of a specified element, precisely implementing the mechanism of tree element selection.

For an example, we may refer again to Fig. 2 (p. 18) and suppose that $X2$ contains the (singular) address of the codeword Q. Then the instruction:

$$X1 \quad LOAD \quad X2$$

causes the value of Q to be fetched into $X1$ (with the precaution that its tag is 2). The limit value (m) in $X1$ is now 5, and the type code (t) is 8. $X1$ therefore has tag 2(8) and refers to a sequence of six absolute codewords. If the next instructions obeyed are:

$$X1 \quad MOD \quad 4$$
$$X1 \quad LIM \quad 0$$

then $X1$ becomes a singular address referring to the fifth element of the set Q. The same effect as the above three orders could be achieved by:

$$X1 \quad COPY \quad X2$$
$$X1 \quad DOT \quad 4$$

If we continue:

$$X1 \quad DOT \quad 1$$
$$X1 \quad LOAD \quad X1$$

44

then the result in *X1* is the address of the set *F*; in a data transfer the codeword *F* would be locked out (tag 1(5)), and the last instruction would not be completed until the transfer had terminated and caused the tag to be reset to 2. In order to search for the first nonzero element of *F* the following loop may be used:

$$
\begin{array}{lll}
X2 & LOAD & X1 \\
NZ & JUMP & 3 \\
X1 & JNL & -2
\end{array}
$$

(continue here if all elements zero)
(continue here if element found)

The first instruction loads a value into *X2* by A/F, and sets the condition indicators, which are tested by the next instruction. The third instruction tests to see if *X1* is singular; if not it modifies *X1* by 1 and jumps back to the first instruction; if *X1* is singular (or 'last'), the next instruction in sequence is obeyed. It should be noted that the above orders are independent of whether the set *F* consists of bytes, words or numeric elements.

The remaining addressing functions are used to enquire the limit value (*INDEX*) and test type (*TTYPE*) and tag (*TTAG*) values in a register by setting condition codes. *MEM* may be used to compare addresses, or more generally to see whether one sequence is contained in, or identical with, another. Tag and type values may be changed by *WTAG* and *WTYPE* respectively, the latter adjusting the limit value if the new type code implies a new size.

3.7 Instruction formats

The list of 39 functions given in Table 3 is extremely comprehensive in comparison with conventional order codes. Its range may be further increased by inventing new data types, e.g. for decimal, complex, or multi-length arithmetic, and by inventing new functions. It seems safe to assume, however, that a six-bit function code (F) will be sufficient for future development. With a four-bit code selecting the first argument (X), ten bits of the instruction are assigned.

The second argument is most frequently a register (Y) or an integer value (N). Assuming N rarely exceeds 16 bits, two instruction formats are suggested, i.e.:

2	6	4	4	
0	F	X	Y	Short

2	6	4	4	16	
1	F	X		± N	Long Literal

45

Two other choices of second argument remain to be made on the basis of coding efficiency. If conventional practice is followed, a 'modifier' address (Y) may be introduced:

| 2 | F | X | Y | + N | Modified Address |

Here the second argument is taken as the singular address formed from Y modified by N with the usual tag and limit comparison. A fourth candidate is a singular address formed relative to *XC*, but with type code T taken from the instruction:

| 3 | F | X | T | ± N | *XC* Relative |

The type T and relative address N are computed by the assembly program. (Only four bits are available for T, but the full range of type values, for which five bits have been assumed, is not necessary in this context.)

The most useful instruction format therefore appears to be 16 or 32 bits in size, the most efficient code being obtained when the second argument is held in a register. Many suboptimisations of the above general pattern are possible, and indeed are assumed to be desirable. The specification of second argument in Basic Language has a more general form, and is matched to the machine code by the action of the translator. In Table 3 the second argument can be assumed to be defined by any of the above formats except where a literal (N) value is specified, in which case either of the first two is used, depending on the size of N.

4

BASIC LANGUAGE

The Basic Machine 'hardware' recognises structure to the extent of sequences of operands of various types, but undisciplined use of the machine order code would not allow the dynamic control of structures and processes which are prime objectives of the engineering model. In the present chapter, the concepts of program and segment structure and of the process hierarchy are introduced, and it is shown how they are realised through the use of Basic Language. For this purpose it is sufficient to present the Language in a very simple form; it is obviously amenable to conventional syntactic extensions providing, for example, a static 'block structure' in program texts, and to various expansion algorithms which make it a more interesting programming tool, but that is beside the point in the current context since the hardware interface is not affected by them.

4.1 Stores

In the BLM, as in most computer systems, there are three sorts of store: the *registers*, which are selected directly by codes in the instructions; the *program store*, which is addressed by implicit or explicit reference to registers; and the *file store*, which can only be processed by transferring its contents to and from the program store.

The file store is a collection of files, where a file is defined as an ordered set of *records*. We shall briefly be concerned with the form of records transferred to the program store, and more particularly with their form when representing Basic Language programs. From outside, part of the file store is apparent to the user of the machine, who must arrange to channel all his information through it. For economic reasons, access to a file is relatively slow. It is made possible by means of stored programs which reflect a more or less complex relationship between files, appropriate to the computer system. It is possible to devise a number of operations, such as copying, merging, sorting or translating, which can be carried out exclusively on files, and to express them in the commands of a file processing language. However, because it is interpretive, and likely to remain so, file manipulation is not strongly affected by details of central processor design, and the file handling operations of Basic

47

Language are not included in the description which follows. The resemblance between certain file structures[14] and the program tree of the Basic Language will be noted, but it is not a particularly useful connection to pursue in detail, since they have different engineering constraints.

Program store

The program store is a tree structure rooted in a single set of codewords constituting the program base. This is the only set not defined by a higher-level codeword; it occupies a fixed sequence of store locations, and any single element can be addressed by the two machine functions provided for that purpose (*JPB*, *LPB*) which in effect supply the implicit tag 2(8) to the location number. The tag and type codes permitted are precisely those of the Basic Machine, in addition to which certain standard interpretations of tag 1 elements are made by escape routines.

In an inactive system the program base always defines a fixed residue of routines and constants necessary for the translation of Basic Language programs, and for the initiation and execution of processes. The routines are invariant, and may be used by several processes at once, but their working space must be separately associated with each user. In the course of calculation a user may add new sets to the program base, retaining their addresses for future reference. A set is said to be *owned* by the process which created it, and the ownership of a codeword set is automatically extended to all its subsets. It follows that at any instant the program store can be partitioned into the permanent residue and a number of nonoverlapping regions owned by the currently active processes. It will be shown later how it is possible for one process to refer to elements owned by another, and to store into any unprotected data set, but to change a *structure* other than one's own is not permitted.

The program store may be distributed over several physical storage media at the discretion of the store control system, in attempting to retain the most frequently used information in the most readily accessible positions. Backing stores, characterised by the property that single bytes or words cannot be retrieved economically, may be integrated by means of the tag 1(6) codeword giving the position and length of a block of information. When such a codeword is accessed, computation is interrupted while the entire block is brought into primary storage (cf. section 2.3). Although such actions are usually automatic, it is possible for the Basic Language programmer to enquire whether a block is in primary storage or not, and to act accordingly. It can also be seen that this form of integration requires that if a set is in primary storage, then so must be all codewords between it and the program base, otherwise difficulties arise in the control of store allocation. The store-conscious programmer would take account of this when estimating his requirements.

Registers

The registers are designated 'X0', 'X1', . . ., 'X9' and correspond to the first ten registers of the Basic Machine. The latter's 'XA', 'XB', . . ., 'XF' are not normally identified, except in a special version of the Language used for writing a small minority of system routines. (Thus the common convention of a privileged execution mode is replaced by a special mode of assembly in the BLM.)

Operations between registers include most of those appearing as Basic Machine functions in Table 3, though the symbolic form of the language often permits several machine functions (e.g. jumps) to be rolled into one. Certain restrictions apply to **TAG** (Table 5) which is constrained to operate only on the integer and numeric tag and type values, and only to generate tag codes 0 and 3, or types N (p. 37). Moreover, 'read-only' status cannot be changed.

The result of the above restrictions is to give programmers control of integer and numeric data representations, but not of address, escape, or instruction codes. Before taking it, however, he is well advised to examine the effects of doing so, for so long as **TAG** is unused he enjoys the same immunity from details of representation as he does from, e.g., address formats, and his programs have correspondingly greater generality. It is not often possible to be independent of integer (tag 0) formats, but the numeric representation (tag 3) could be defined by its arithmetic qualities such as precision, range, and truncation rules, rather than by a binary pattern which it is not necessary to know in order to program effectively. Such is the situation in most programs written in high-level languages, and one of the sources of their generality; it is also known that if a language allows a change of type coding, e.g. by remapping a common data area, then some programs making use of that feature will be restricted to run on machines with identical numeric representation. The existence of such languages, and of problems with extreme numerical sensitivity, forces the Basic Language to admit type and tag conversion, but not without a word of caution.

The registers also provide the arguments for a group of executive functions, E, which is realised by permanent routines in much the same way as 'extracode' or 'executive' functions on conventional machines. Although logically more complex, they are as 'hard' a part of the machine as any other, and it is desirable to conceal their special character. This is achieved by using the two registers XA and XB to communicate parameters; the executive functions are always expressed in one- or two-argument form, and where a 'result' is meaningful it is stored to a destination given by the first argument.

49

The assembly program distinguishes group E from others, and inserts orders copying arguments into *XA* and *XB*. Certain functions require more than two arguments, or possibly a variable number, in which case a sequence of them is formed in the register stack (by *DUMP* instructions) and the address of the sequence is placed in *XA* or *XB* as appropriate. The executive routine can discriminate between the various possibilities by using *TTAG*, *TTYPE* and *INDEX* instructions, and act accordingly.

From the programmers' point of view, the registers will be seen as part of the process base, the elements of which have almost the same logical properties. However, it is to be assumed that explicit use of registers will generally give faster and more compact code.

4.2 Processes

A process is defined as the act of performing a sequence of Basic Language instructions, selected by given control functions and escape actions. Whether the process is implemented in a multi-programming or multiprocessing environment is outside the scope of the engineering model. A unique base is associated with each process, through which it gains access to the program store, but not to other bases. The base elements also provide connections with the file storage system, by means of file addresses (tag 1(7)).

A primary requirement of a multiprogramming machine is that at least one process should be active and capable of controlling others. In the BLM, this is termed the *system process* (π_0). If we adopt the principle of equating system activities with others as far as possible, it follows that all processes should have the ability to create and interact with certain others. We now examine the conditions to be satisfied if calculation is to proceed effectively.

It is easily possible for a free community of processes, each empowered to influence any other, to degenerate into chaos. A fairly strict bound on the number of interactions which can take place would therefore be acceptable. Indeed, the first guiding principle is that if a programmer chooses to write a single process, free from consideration of all others, he should be able to do so. This is by far the most common practical requirement. One loophole must be left, however, to enable a controlling process to intervene in case of unexpected errors or external interruptions, and it is sufficient that each process should have just one such *supervisor* (though the system process is exceptional in having none), and not to admit control from any other process.

We describe as a *subprocess* of π_j any process of which π_j is the supervisor. The Basic Language provides orders for initiating and terminating subprocesses, and for controlling their intermediate states. The number of subprocesses is restricted only by the resourcefulness of the supervisor, because the resources required by each subprocess are subtracted from those available to the supervisor. For example, the primary storage allotted to a supervisor can never be exceeded by the total requirements of its subprocesses, but whether this is monitored by budgeting for a certain amount when each is started, or by pooling the demands of several subprocesses, can be left to the discretion of the programmer. Competition for shared services, such as channel capacity, is normally resolved in the interest of overall system performance.

The familiar picture of a 'process tree' structure can be seen looming over the horizon, and there is some temptation to look for it in the program store itself. However, there is no particular reason why control relationships should be reflected in the store structure, especially as they are handled interpretively. The only tangible evidence of a process hierarchy is the supervisor number, and list of subprocesses, to be found in each process base in positions only accessible to system routines.

Store sharing

It is a common practical requirement that a subprocess should have access to at least part of its supervisor's store. The convention is adopted of permitting a process to search its supervisor's base for a named element, and so on up to the level of π_0 or until a match is found; if it is, the element is copied into the current base; if not, an undefined element is created in its place. No restrictions are placed on access to invariant information, but in the case of an unprotected data set, for example, the supervisor needs some say in whether it can be shared and, if so, whether it should be protected from the subprocess by changing it to the read-only type code; this facility would normally be provided in some form of declarative statement.

4.3 Pragmatics

The description of a language intended for both on-line and off-line use, controlling both scalar and nonscalar quantities, and for program development as well as execution, has to meet considerations which set it apart from conventional machines or higher-level languages.

The first objective of Basic Language is to operate on the program and file stores and the process hierarchy. It is straightforward to define functions for this purpose and to express them symbolically with their arguments in the form of instructions. A sequence of operations can be expressed in the form of a sequence of instructions, i.e. a file whose elements (records) are byte sets conforming to the rules of the Language.

It is then necessary to distinguish between *direct* sequences and *indirect* ones. In the latter, instructions may be labelled, and a general sequencing rule allowing labels as jump destinations is adopted, since it is assumed that the entire sequence will be translated and assigned (in binary form) to the program store before it is obeyed. In the former case, only a limited number of instructions (possibly one) is retained and the sequencing rule is restricted accordingly.

Allowance must also be made for the probability that a process is described by many separate sequences of instruction, written by different programmers and separately translated into binary form. A *program segment* is such a sequence of instructions, though its definition is widened to include data and relative codeword blocks at any level of the tree. It is translated into a single block in storage; to change its internal structure it must be retranslated from symbolic text, whereas in the program as a whole one block may be changed for another at any time. This state of affairs is reflected in the recognition of two classes of identifier, the *local* and *global names*, which address the current segment and the process base respectively, though except in operations effecting structural changes their use is quite symmetrical.

In miniature, segment substructure parallels the program tree structure. Its coding has much the same character as the single block of program in a von Neumann machine, except that the distinction between instructions and data is preserved, and the data structure itself is formalised by relative codewords. It is not strictly necessary to preserve the tree structure within a segment provided the assembler can handle the chosen referencing system, but one important practical consideration is that the binary form of a segment should be reversible into symbolic code in order to present intelligible diagnostic information, and by retaining the tree structure this is achieved relatively easily.

The intended mode of machine operation is one in which processes are developed over long or short time intervals, making extensive use of the variable structure of the program and file stores to accommodate problem changes. The method of constructing binary coded segments is crucial to the success of such a scheme. They must not only be independent of physical location, but also permit efficient communication with other segments, under shared or non-shared conditions, and require the minimum of maintenance from the system once they have been assembled. These considerations significantly affect the form of segments and executive functions, which is discussed in the next two subsections.

4.4 Program segments

Syntactic definitions are given in the Appendix and exemplified in the remainder of the present chapter. Any Basic Language expression can be 'evaluated' at three distinguishable levels, i.e. syntactic, type comparison, and AutoFetch. At each level the evaluation may 'fail' and lead to assembly, tag conflict, or invalid result monitoring, but the stage of evaluation at which monitoring occurs will depend on the sophistication of the translator. In the Basic Language function list (Table 5) the rules of syntax and type are summarised, from which it will be clear that certain type evaluations could be carried out 'syntactically' with suitable elaboration of formats; whether or not this is done is not specified in the engineering model.

A program segment is a sequence of data and instruction definitions, normally written on successive lines, and represented by a data file. If β is the address of such a file, then its execution by process α as a direct sequence can be initiated by an instruction of the form:

$$\alpha \quad \textbf{CIS} \quad \beta$$

(CIS stands for Command Input Stream.) This instruction is normally implied when any new input document is presented to the system, in which case β may be omitted, although different interpretations can be specified by the user. The normal action is intended to allow control of processes by Basic Language instructions input, for example, at keyboards or paper-tape readers.

A file is thus interpreted initially in the direct mode. It may be switched at any time to indirect by means of the function **SEG** which appears as:

$$\eta \quad \textbf{SEG} \quad \mu$$

where η is a compound name denoting an absolute codeword, and μ is a non-negative integer giving the number of *entry points* to the block about to be assembled and stored at η. Translation continues in indirect mode until the function **END** is encountered.

Within an indirect segment definition, all data definitions must be labelled (otherwise they cannot be used), and instructions may be labelled when used as jump destinations. Data and instructions may be mixed in the program text, but normal control sequencing passes from one instruction to the next without attempting to 'obey' intervening data. Relative jumps may be expressed either by labels or by line counts relative to the current instruction, but the latter method is recommended for short jumps only. A single Basic Language instruction is translated into one or more Basic Machine instructions, the relative line count being adjusted by the assembly program.

The practice of distinguishing formally between different categories of identifiers is introduced here to simplify the presentation rather than as a permanent feature of the Language. Thus a *global name* is a register name or one of 'A', 'B', ..., 'Z', corresponding to elements of the extended register store (not necessarily in that order). A *local name* can only be defined within the segment, e.g. as an instruction label; it may be entirely private, in which case one of the letters 'a',

53

'b', ..., 'z' is used for it, or it may also be referred to from another segment, when it is denoted by '#0', '#1', ..., '#n', $n + 1$ being the number of entry points. Since a global name denotes an element of the process base, its value is variable; a local name, on the other hand, denotes a fixed address, which is absorbed into XC-relative instructions.

Compound names

The formation of global and local names may be compared with the conventional assembly program practice of allowing symbols to be associated with single locations in a linear store. In the BLM, however, only a fraction of the store is so addressed; any other element must be selected by giving the indices of elements in a path leading to it from a specified base position. For this purpose, the notation of the 'dot' operator has already been used (p. 19). In Basic Language, any global or local name is accepted as a compound name; also, an expression consisting of a compound name, then a dot, then a non-negative integer, is a compound name, e.g.:

'X6', '#3', 'Y', '#1.6', 'X4.0.3'

The expression is said to be locally or globally based according to the category of the first component. If **A** (say) is a segment with three entry points, they are referred to as #0, #1, #2, within the text of **A**, but any other segment refers to them as 'A.0', 'A.1', and 'A.2'. In certain contexts the null symbol 'Ω' is admitted as a compound name, representing a tag 1(0) element.

In terms of a conceptual tree structure, a compound name η refers to a (possibly singular) sequence of elements. If the first element defines a set, then compound names of the form 'η.0', 'η.1', ..., etc. may be used to refer to the elements of that set; if it does not, the derived compound names are invalid. The **DOT** function has been designed to mechanise the path selection process exactly, and to fail when the compound name is invalid.

For practical purposes, the definition of a compound name would be extended to admit notations equivalent to the other addressing functions (**MOD, LIM,** and **LOAD**) and to generalise the path description by allowing variable indices, evaluated at execution time. The advantage of doing so is that it allows operations on sequences to be expressed concisely, but the same results can be achieved in the present context by using separate instructions. Essentially the same principle is invoked when expressions involving arithmetic operators are admitted in place of single variables.

Labels

The form of a label is that of a locally based compound name immediately followed by a colon. If the name has more than one component, then at each addressing level a relative codeword set must have been declared previously in the program text. For example, a compound name such as #3.5 in the line:

>#3.5 : X2 ADD 3

is only acceptable if a preceding line defines #3 as a relative codeword set with limit at least 5 (see below).

Definition of local constants

A label followed by an integer defines a local constant, which if nonzero is given 'read-only' status. It is also permitted to represent small sets of various types by a list of numerical terms separated by commas and enclosed in parentheses:

>**p : (0, 12, 1077, –8)**   *A set of 4 words (type 2)*
>**q : (0, 12, 67)**   *A set of 3 bytes (type 3)*

The use of parentheses can be extended to multiline definitions, and to the description of tree structures in a natural way, but these possibilities are not elaborated here. A set of zero or null elements of a given type is frequently required, and may conveniently be expressed in the form '$[n_1 : n_2]$' where n_1 and n_2 are numerals representing the set type and limit respectively, e.g.:

>**r : [9 : 5]**   *A set of 6 undefined relative codewords*

The acceptable values of n_1 are 0, 1, 9, 12 and 13 in this context. After such a definition, further subsets may be defined within the same program segment, e.g.:

>**r.0 : [0 : 99]**   *A set of 100 zero words*
>**r.3 : X6 SUB 7**   *Program entry point*

and so on. The order of definition of subsets is immaterial. A further option is to indicate that the set should be extended on modification overflow by using the semicolon in place of colon as separator, as in '[0 ; 79]'. Such a set is automatically extended by 80 elements whenever modification overflow occurs.

A list of locally based compound names, separated by commas and enclosed in parentheses, is termed a *constant name set*. It is represented by a set of relative codewords, and provides a special mapping within a single segment, e.g.:

>**#2: (#1, r, u.3)** *A set of three relative codewords.*

Such expressions are particularly intended for local switches. Multiple references are allowed.

More generally, a finite sequence of elements may be expressed as any list of constants or compound names, represented by elements of mixed type (11). For certain elements there is no direct representation, and recourse must be made to Basic Machine code, i.e. 'soft' interpretation (type 1(8)), though this, like the instruction code itself, is a negotiable part of the logical design.

In Basic Language commands, constants may be used in any context where a protected singular address is meaningful. For example:

$$\text{X3} \quad \text{LOAD} \quad \text{(a, b, c)}$$

results with **X3** as the address of a sequence of three relative code-words, i.e. tag 2(9), limit 2. Such expressions may conveniently be used to convey lists of parameters between different parts of a program.

Instructions

The reservation of *XA* and *XB* for assembled code allows the arguments of most instructions to be generalised to compound names, numerical constants, or sets, whenever it is sensible to do so. A constant is represented by its address, and a set by the address of its codeword; the use of such arguments as destinations would lead to failure at the AutoStore level, but this is clearly one of the cases referred to above where appropriate checks can be made during assembly.

Arithmetic functions correspond exactly with Group A of the Basic Machine. The arguments can be any compound names or constants. For example, the Basic Language instruction:

$$\text{X6} \quad \text{ADD} \quad \text{s.3}$$

is translated into Basic Machine codes:

$$\begin{array}{lll} XB & COPY & XC\,(s)\ (T = 9) \\ XB & DOT & 3 \\ X6 & ADD & XB \end{array}$$

The first machine instruction uses the *XC* relative format, *s* being the relative address of **s**, and the type code (9) indicates that **s** is a relative codeword. Such expressions tend to generate rather loose coding, but they may be justified in certain circumstances, on much the same grounds as other expansion techniques. The AutoFetch rules for elements of mixed type are designed to help indirect operations on the process base.

A general facility is provided for using a function only to set condition indicators (*c*) and not to store the result; it is invoked by following the function identifier with an asterisk, e.g.:

$$\text{X3} \quad \text{SUB*} \quad \text{X6}$$

which is translated as:

$$X3 \quad TEST \quad X6$$

but a less frequently used test option such as:

$$\text{X4} \quad \text{ADD*} \quad \text{5}$$

would be translated by first copying $X4$ into XB. All implied type conversions are assumed in the setting of c. Functions admitting this variant are marked * in Table 5.

Generalised arguments are not possible for functions operating wholly or partly on addresses (corresponding to Groups B, D in the Machine), to which AutoFetch is not applicable. In such cases the operand is generally a base element, and is therefore selected by a global name. It will be recalled (p. 54) that the set of (singular) addresses corresponding to local names is implicit, and therefore cannot be used as a destination of a result. However, such names may be used as sources, and copied into base positions where they may be operated on, e.g.:

A   COPY   r

A   DOT   2

In order to operate on elements of a mixed set, the programmer must use **RF** and **RS** functions, corresponding to the machine codes. It will be noted that special formats are retained for functions requiring an integer second argument (**MON, RET**) and for **TAG, DUMP** and **UNDUMP**, which are simple generalisations of the corresponding machine functions.

The only functions for which register arguments cannot be simply generalised to the entire process base are control jumps (Group C), because once the jump is taken it is necessary to obey the **RS** order which would normally be required to return XA or XB to the extended register store. The first argument of **JUMP** (if it exists) serves to distinguish four subcases, i.e.

First argument X : jump and set link in X, as in:

X6   JUMP   5

First argument condition mnemonic : conditional jump, as in:

ZE   JUMP   t

First argument integer constant : jump and store marked link, as in:

3   JUMP   A.5

First argument blank : unconditional jump.

JUMP   −3

The jump destination may be a relative line count (as in the first and last examples above), to a local label (as in the second example) or, more generally, to any compound name, which must be represented by a tag 2(I) element or the address of one.

Representing program segments

The task of representing segment substructure in Basic Machine code is not significantly different from that faced by a conventional single-pass assembly program. The availability of XC and XD enables the address of any global or local name to be formed from the corresponding index. It is possible to use a name before its index is known, and before it is known which base address to use (though our present notation prevents this), but provided the actual space requirement is the same in either case it is comparatively easy to fill in the unknown addresses by a chaining technique at a later stage of assembly. In the case of local (segment) names, this also involves filling in type codes (see Section 3.7, XC relative format).

However, as was noted in Chapter 2, the index of a global name is normally unknown at assembly time, since the segment may be intended for use in a different environment, and a mechanism must be provided for completing the external connections when it is brought into use. There are two possibilities to consider:

If the segment is nonsharable then the store routines can write the correct base indices into the segment when it is loaded into its operating environment, either by using a connection table or by modification of XD. If such a segment is copied within the same environment no difficulty arises, but if it is written to file store care must be taken to re-establish symbolic cross-references the next time it is used, since the process base indices may have changed.

The second possibility is that the segment is shared, or at least sharable. This could be assumed from the absence of unprotected data definitions, and it is therefore recognised by the translator. Then the symbolic connection must be made by escape interpretation of an element in the connection table each time a global name is used. As noted in Chapter 2, the inefficiency inherent in this technique may be mitigated by carrying out the table search once on entering a routine, and retaining the resulting address in the registers or stack while it is needed.

4.5 Executive functions (Group E)

The executive functions are designed to create and control the information structure recognised in Basic Language, namely the program and file stores, and the process hierarchy. They are therefore divided into three subgroups which we discuss separately, listing only a minimum of functions in each.

Program store control

A notation for constant and variable sets, including sets of zeros or tag 1 elements, was introduced in the previous subsection. The primary objective of store control is to be able to 'assign' such sets, when needed, to selected branches of the program store. This function is performed by **EQU** (Equals). The destination is normally the address of an absolute codeword, which is to be overwritten by the codeword defining the new set. Thus the instruction:

M   EQU   [8:5]

defines **M** as the address of a codeword defining a set of 6 absolute codewords with tag 1(0). Two possible situations must be considered:

(a) **M** is initially represented by the address of an absolute codeword, and therefore has tag 2(8). In this case the action is to overwrite the existing codeword.

(b) In all other cases, a new codeword is added to the program base, containing the set definition, and addressed by **M**. For example if **X6** is null, then:

X6   EQU   [13:99]
X6   LD   X6

places the long address of a new sequence of 100 short numeric elements in X6.

It can be seen that the interpretation of **EQU** is partly analogous to that of **MOVE** with AutoStore.

In case (a), the rule of ownership to which we have already referred is applied, and the function fails if **M** refers to a codeword not owned by the current process. In case (b), the resulting set is, by definition, owned by the current process. The successful execution of **EQU** involves more or less work in finding sufficient storage space, depending on the character of the problem and concurrent workload. Some of the practical considerations are discussed in Chapter 5, but it is obvious that the programmer at Basic Language level can never be entirely absolved from considerations of store economics, and the Language itself provides the tools for handling a wide variety of strategies.

Stored structures may be defined on the basis of an existing codeword set, defined as above. Thus we may extend **M** by instructions of the form:

M.3   EQU   [1:39]

Definitions may also be made by copying an existing structure:

A   EQU   M.3

Note that the **COPY** function itself copies only a single (tagged) word, i.e.:

B   COPY   M.3

59

has the effect of placing the address of **M.3** into the base position corresponding to **B** (Fig. 5).

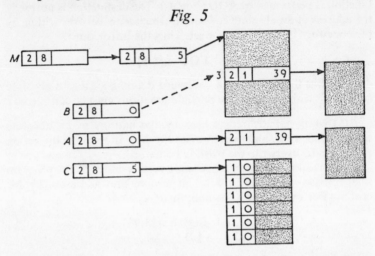

Fig. 5

The function **SEG**, introduced at the beginning of Section 4.4, is similar in interpretation to **EQU**, except that it is always obeyed directly, and defines a single block of information in accordance with the rules of the Language.

A number of functions can be derived from **EQU** in order to replicate all or part of a structure. For example, one might base a function for copying only the *first* level of a tree on the following code sequence, which is written to apply to **M** and **C**:

```
M    TAG*    2(8)
NZ   JUMP    6
X1   LOAD    M
X2   INDEX   X1
X3   TYPE    X1
C    EQU     [X3:X2]
     RET     0
C    TAG     1(0)
     RET     1
```

The length of a set is altered by inserting elements before a given position. This is normally a time-consuming procedure unless a special (chained) representation is used, as described in Chapter 5. Then an instruction such as:

M.6 INSERT 40

causes 40 elements to be inserted in the set **M** after the sixth element (i.e. before **M.6**). If the second argument is negative, elements are

60

removed, starting at the given position, and all addresses adjusted accordingly. In order to add elements to the end of a set, it is possible (and advantageous) to use modification overflow detection to increase the set length automatically using the notation introduced on p. 55. In this way the programmer does not have to test for the end of a data set when he increases its length. Under these conditions, it should be noted that **JL** and **JNL** refer to the current set limit and do not cause any increase in length.

File store control

Attachment to the file store is explicitly programmed by means of an **OPEN** instruction, whose first operand is a global name (β) and second operand is a file name (ϕ). The effect of **OPEN** is to search all available files for one with a name equivalent (in some predetermined sense) to ϕ, and then to store a file address at the position corresponding to β in the process base. Subsequent control is effected by using the global name β; the file address contains information enabling system routines to identify the particular device giving access to the file, its relative position, mode of transfer, and operational status. By suitable interpretation of ϕ, **OPEN** can also be used to create new files. The file attachment is automatically severed when there are no addresses referring to it.

There are two *modes* of record transfer, the mode of a file being fixed at the time of its creation. The first is the *data mode*, the files to which it applies are *data files*, and it corresponds closely with conventional practice of transmitting sequences of elementary binary quantities between a buffer in core store and an external device. The buffer is defined by giving the address of a tag 2(N) codeword, and the device is defined by a file address. In Basic Language, the position of the arguments relative to the **TFER** function is taken to define the direction of flow of information, from the second argument to the first, e.g. if α has tag 2(8(N)) and β has tag 1(7):

α **TFER** β *Inputs a block, and*
β **TFER** α *Outputs a block*

The data mode of transfer is inapplicable to sets of instructions or codewords, one reason being that it would violate the protection rules of the system to allow arbitrary binary data to be read in and classified as instructions. The second mode is introduced to handle such information; it is called the *structured mode*, and the files to which it applies are *structured files*. The source or destination in core store can be defined by any tagged element. The information written to the file is the entire structure defined by the element, *including* the structural information itself (if the codeword is 'undefined', a recognisable 'null' record is written). When a record is read from a structured file the information in the record is used to reconstruct exactly the pattern of data, instructions, and codewords from which it was formed. In this way part of the program store can be saved and recovered for use at a later time.

It will be seen, again for security reasons, that any file prepared by the user must be in data mode; structured files are mainly a means of intermediate storage, though they may also be used in generating interpreted diagnostic output.

In most other respects, the Basic Machine file control system offers facilities similar to a conventional machine's. Functions are required for 'positioning' the file address to transmit a particular record, to create and destroy files, to rename them and to act upon failures. The functions already defined for operating on the program store (**EQU, INSERT**) and addresses (**MOD, DOT, TAG**, etc.) find parallels in the file system to a greater or less degree depending on its approximation to a tree structure, but, as already noted, detailed definitions are liable to diverge to take account of the physical characteristics of input and output devices.

Process control

A subprocess is created by the operation **PROC**, whose first operand is a global name, and second operand is a process name (π). Interpretation of π determines the method of resource allocation and accounting, and may also allow a dormant process to be revived from file storage. Subsequent control of the process is effected by using the assigned global name, which has tag 1(9).

Since a process may already be active when a **CIS** command is addressed to it, a system of priorities must be applied to determine whether to permit an interruption, how to service the queue of command streams which could be built up, and how to resume an interrupted calculation. For most practical purposes a single interrupt level is sufficient to control a subprocess, but further research in this area is necessary before a firm engineering interface can be specified.

4.6 An example

To illustrate some Basic Language programming conventions we consider a simple table-forming routine **T** and a program **Q** to test it. The table entries are either words or bytes, stored in ascending index positions starting with the second element. The first element contains the index value of the last position occupied at any time, and is initially set to zero.

Control is transferred to **T** with a mark 1 link in the register stack, with the table codeword's address in **X0**, and the argument value or its address in **X1**. On exit, the argument value is replaced by its index in the table. The argument is entered in the table if not already present; the table is extended by means of an assumed interpretation of modification overflow when it is full. Since it uses only the register stack for intermediate storage, **T** is invariant and therefore sharable.

The first input text causes **T** to be translated to binary form and written to the file store at address ϕ_1. It is assumed that the text is input to the system process (π_0), so it begins by starting a subprocess (π_1) which is referred to as 'Q' by π_0. The first two commands are obeyed directly by π_0, and the next one by π_1:

Q	PROC	π_1	*Initiate new process*
Q	CIS		*Give command stream to* **Q**
T	SEG	0	*Begin definition of* **T**

The next lines are translated indirectly by **Q** in the course of building up **T**. The (single) entry point is labelled #0:

#0 :	DUMP	X0, X1, X2	
X0	LOAD	X0	*Form table address*
X1	LOAD	X1	*Evaluate argument*
X2	COPY	X0	*Save table address*
X0	LIM	X0	*Limit table address*

Note that in the last instruction, A/F applies to the second argument (to find the current limit in the first position of the table) but not to the first, which is an address. The table scan and action on finding a match are now:

X0	JL	w	*Test for end and modify* **X0**
X0	TEST	X1	*A/F applies to 1st argument*
NZ	JUMP	−2	
X0	MEM	X2	*Find current index of* **X0** *in* **X2**
e :	UNDUMP	X2, X1	*Replace* **X1, X2**
X1	MOVE	X0	*Store result*
	UNDUMP	X0	*Replace* **X0**
	RET	1	*Exit via link in stack*

The next instructions deal with the situation where no match has been found:

w :	X2	ADD	1	*Increase entry count in table*
	X0	LOAD	X2	*Index of new element*
	X2	MOD	X2	*(Extend table if overflow)*
	X2	MOVE	X1	*Store new entry*
		JUMP	e	*Jump to exit sequence*
END				*End of* **T**

The command input now reverts to direct mode in order to file the assembled block and terminate command input.

	F	OPEN	ϕ_1	*Form file address* **F**
	F	TFER	T	*Output assembled segment*
END				*End of command input to* **Q**

The second text recalls **T** from the file store and subjects it to two tests with trial values **S**, forming tables of results **P**. The routine **R** applies **T** to successive arguments from **S**. A visible display of results is assumed in file ϕ_2. The text starts off as before and then defines **R**.

	Q	PROC	π_1	
	Q	CIS		
	R	SEG	0	
#0 :	V	TFER	S	*Output test data*
	X0	COPY	P	*Table address*
	X1	LOAD	S	*Argument addresses*
	1	JUMP	T	*Apply* **T** *to first argument*
	X1	JNL	−1	*Modify through arguments*
	V	TFER	S	*Output indices*
	V	TFER	P	*Output table*
		JUMP	X2	*Return to link in register*
END				*End of* **R**

The remainder of the second text is concerned with defining the output file, recalling **T**, and presenting test data. Since **T** overwrites its argument values, they cannot be presented as constant, i.e. protected sets. We here assume an escape interpretation of **MOVE** which copies one set into another, element by element.

	V	OPEN	ϕ_2	*Define output file*
	F	OPEN	ϕ_1	
	T	TFER	F	*Recall* **T** *to program store*
	P	EQU	[0;9]	*Define table space (extending)*
	S	EQU	[1:5]	
	S	MOVE	(1,3,2,3,3,4)	*First test data*
	X2	JUMP	R	*Jump to first test*
	S	MOVE	(5,6,7,8,9,10)	*Second test data*
	X2	JUMP	R	*Jump to second test*
END				*End of Command Input*
	Q	TAG	1	*Abolish* **Q**

5

TECHNIQUES

It was noted in the first chapter that the essential qualities of the Basic Machine derive from its ability to recognise greater structural details in programs than can be found in conventional computers, and that the derived benefits must be weighed against certain disadvantages. It is clear from Chapter 3, however, that the mechanisation of the instruction code presents no extraordinary problems. The examination of tags effectively turns the six-bit function code into twelve, with a regularity which can be exploited in logical design. The detailed limit comparisons carried out by addressing functions correspond to the address checking demanded of any multiprogramming machine (and it should be noticed that on the Basic Machine the check is made only when an address is formed by modification, and not every time it is used to access the store). The intervention of the Basic Language assembly program allows any function to be expanded into an open subroutine or an executive function call whenever it is uneconomical to include it in the machine logic. And in conventional applications of the machine, any extra store cycles caused by stepping down the tree structure are more than offset by the compactness of the order code and the consequent saving in instruction accesses.

In order to find more conspicuous disadvantages in the codeword system one must therefore turn to the cost of maintaining the tree structure, which is borne by the system, and of writing a program to operate on it, which is borne by the user. Thus, on the assumption that all store maintenance is unproductive work carried out to the exclusion of useful calculation, one can form some idea of its cost, and the main system parameters affecting it. That this is an extreme upper limit follows from considering the two objectives of the store control system: firstly to provide the store structure chosen by a programmer with, one must assume, some beneficial return in mind; secondly to integrate the primary storage with backing stores of various kinds, a service which must be provided by some means in all machines. However, one can predict the most unfavourable circumstances and provide a range of techniques for bringing their costs within the bounds of conventional practice. In the present chapter, we examine how this is done, and note the restrictions remaining on programming.

5.1 Store control in general

In its simplest form, storage allocation in any medium requires that the available units of storage be classified as either *active* or *inactive*, and that requests for space be satisfied by searching the inactive store for a unit of sufficient length, part of which is then transferred to active status. This process can continue until the search fails, when more or less violent steps must be taken to replenish the inactive space. Such a situation is familiar to anyone who has packed a suitcase; rather than postpone his holiday, he would have recourse to one of the less drastic measures, i.e.:

(a) reorganise the existing allocation in order to make available larger inactive units, e.g. by moving all active elements to one end of the store;

(b) eject certain elements to a different storage medium (e.g. the Baggage Room), normally on the basis of a measure of *usage* which is reflected in system performance; and

(c) add to the inactive space by considering the ownership of active elements, and reclaiming them as soon as the owning process terminates (it is assumed that a process cannot terminate while it still has subprocesses). The traveller meets this situation when half his party decides not to go after all.

In the Basic Machine, the storage elements vary in length from one byte to 2^{16} double-length words. The inactive store can therefore be represented as a set I of byte sets, and the search for a block length of limit at least X1 becomes:

X0	LOAD	I	*Address of inactive sequence*
X2	LOAD	X0	*Address of first element*
X2	INDEX	X2	*Find length*
X2	SUB*	X1	*Compare*
GE	JUMP	f	f : *found*
X0	JNL	−4	*Repeat if too small*

(In a high-performance machine, this loop would probably be carried out in a single instruction.) The cost attributable to scanning the inactive sets is almost directly proportional to the average number of sets to be examined before succeeding, and that in turn is determined by the concurrent work of all processes. In the extreme case where all sets are equal in length the search must succeed at once provided I is not empty, but this condition is impractical when the conceptual block length shows great variation, with the average much less than the maximum. An alternative is to allocate space in multiples of a fixed block size, in order to eliminate the handling

66

of small parcels of storage, at the expense of rounding up each space request to the next integral block. Exactly what the fixed block size should be depends on local circumstances, and provided the allocation is handled by system routines it can be adjusted until an optimum is reached. Another technique, which may be combined with the first, is to define several inactive sets, classified by the length of elements they contain, in order to reduce the scan. In general, however, the temptation towards more elaborate store control algorithms should be modulated by the fact that under average running conditions store requests are relatively infrequent events, and that it is better to carry out wholesale adjustments at times chosen by the operating system than to consume the users' time with detailed book-keeping operations.

Reorganisation

The ideal situation in which each space request can be satisfied in a few tens of instructions, and the inactive store replenished by the natural decay of processes, is likely to be found only in very large or specialised systems. When the search for store fails, but the *total* inactive space is sufficient to meet a request, then it may be satisfied by a partial reallocation of active storage. As noted in Chapter 2, when an active block is moved all addresses pointing into it (including its codeword) must be updated, and therefore the tagged store of its owner and all the owner's subprocesses must be scanned for such addresses. Thus when a single block is re-allocated to make space for another, or as the result of an **INSERT** or modification extension (p. 55) the cost is roughly proportional to the sum of the block length and tagged store index at that instant. When several blocks are moved the cost associated with each is proportional to the block length plus the number of *addresses* in the tagged store, so there is a slight advantage in organising mass movements.

Usage

A measure of usage can be defined for the Basic Machine in the following way. Any sequence of elements whose address is in the process base is given a 'U value' of one. A codeword with U value v ascribes to the set it defines the value $v + 1$, except for sequences addressed directly. In this way each accessible element of the program store is given a unique U value ranging from one up to the maximum depth of the tree. It can be seen that inaccessible elements will result from clearing a process base or from overwriting base elements, e.g. as the result of:

X6	TAG	1	*Clear* X6
X6	EQU	[0:19]	*A set of* 20 *words*
X6	LOAD	10	*Overwrite address*

67

the elements of the set defined by the second instruction are inaccessible, and may be made inactive.

Assuming that the instruction generators have taken rational steps towards shortening address paths, an interpretation of U values which keeps the lowest in the most rapidly accessible stores will tend to reinforce the optimisation already attempted and to increase system performance. Thus, elements with U value one, together with process bases, should be retained in the fastest store, but sets with value two or more are candidates for ejection to slower media if reorganisation cannot meet a store request. A useful rule is to eject all except absolute codewords sets, whose presence in primary storage simplifies control of the secondary store. A refinement is periodically to mark each absolute codeword with a tag 1 in such a way that when it is used the escape action is to reset the tag to 2 and continue. In this way sets which have not been accessed in a given period can be chosen for ejection before the others.

Process suspension

If a space request cannot be satisfied at once, then in a multi-programming system the requesting process would normally be halted until the next reorganisation or ejection phase. If the request still cannot be satisfied, and all processes are halted, the last resort is to suspend one or more processes by writing all the sets they own to a backing store. Each address is converted to a backing store address. The bases themselves can also be ejected provided arrangements are made for updating references to files and supervisors' stores. The processes remain suspended until the system finds time and space to reinstate them.

5.2 Special representations

The frequency of reorganisation and the cost of moving store blocks can be reduced by special techniques using the fact that address formats are concealed from Basic Language programmers. Two of them are described here. They will be seen to involve special ways of codeword evaluation and modification which can be incorporated in the machine logic in the same way as the relative codewords already introduced in Chapter 3.

Chain codewords

The implications of the **INSERT** function are considerably reduced if the sequence to which it is applied is held in chained form rather than in a block of consecutive store locations. That is to say, the successor of each element should be located explicitly rather than by adding a count of one, four or eight to its location number. Absolute codeword sets are well suited to supplying a successor's (double word) location number n in the 'spare' sixteen bits of the word. The last element has a 'zero' successor location.

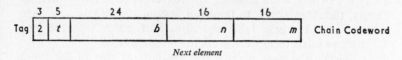

Next element

In other respects the coding is identical with a 'linear' codeword. References to a chained codeword sequence use a special type code (instead of the usual value 8), detected by the modifying functions, which use the chain of addresses to step from one element to the next.

Insertion and deletion of elements is a comparatively painless operation on a chained set, provided no attempt is made to adjust limit values to the new structure. In practice the codeword limit is set to a large value ($2^{16} - 1$) and the end of the set is usually detected by *JL* or *JNL* on the last element. However, *LIM* may also be used to form the address of a subchain. The programmer cannot be entirely oblivious of whether a set is chained or linear, and at the assembly-language level it is at least debatable whether he should. The advantage of chains is that they provide great structural flexibility without going outside the conventions of the language. The price is paid in the slowness of modification, but this is still a machine function, and is appreciably faster than that which has been endured in list processing systems for conventional machines (though chains are not logically the same as lists).

Paged storage

The cost of reorganisation is partly attributable to the physical movement of information from one store area to another. This can be reduced substantially if the primary store is divided into a number of equal-size pages, indirectly addressed through a page table. The only physical reorganisation that is then necessary is in the page table itself.

Consider, for example, a core store of 2^{18} bytes divided into 2^{10} pages of 2^8 bytes each. The first eight pages (2^{10} half-words) are occupied by the page table, and the remaining 1016 pages are available for program storage. The last 1016 half-words of the page table each contain a *page address* which is the ten most significant digits of a page of program storage, and each page address is unique.

Page address

Page Table Element

A location number, as found in a tag 2 element, is now split into a low-order eight bits, giving a byte location, and a high-order sixteen (only ten of which are significant), selecting a page table entry. In theory, therefore, access to the store is gained by obtaining a page address from the page table and using it, together with the byte location, to select an element from the program store.

In practice the page address p is retained as part of the tag 2 word, and it is only necessary to access the page table again if, by modification, b crosses a page boundary. At all other times, addressing is direct.

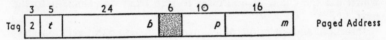

The store control techniques previously applied to the whole store can now be adapted to the page table itself. All space requests are rounded up to a whole number of pages. The inactive page addresses are marked, e.g. by storing them in complemented form, and the scan for space involves searching the page table for the required number of consecutive inactive pages. If the scan fails, reorganisation is applied by moving active page addresses from one part of the table to another, updating all codewords and addresses as usual. Finally, the fixed page length may be exploited in a conventional way to integrate the primary and secondary storage levels.

Virtual stores

The initial advantage of the page table may be pressed further by increasing its length with the aim of reducing the frequency of reorganisation. To gain from doubling the length of table, one must expect to reorganise appreciably less than half as often, because the operation would take twice as long.

In the example given above, we can consider the effect of extending the page table to 2048 half-words (sixteen pages). The program occupies up to 1008 pages of primary storage, the addresses of which are to be found in the page table. The 1040 entries remaining are classified as *free* and are represented by zero. Each table entry is therefore either active, inactive or free (ignoring transient states, and the possibility of referring to backing storage).

The addressing mechanism is unchanged, except that the page table address is increased to eleven significant bits. A store request can be satisfied by finding a sufficient sequence of inactive or free elements, and since over half the table is free the chance of success is substantially higher than before. Before a free element can be used, an inactive page address must be found and copied into it, but this operation consumes very little time. The store control routines therefore face the problem of placing up to 2^{18} bytes in a virtual memory of 2^{19} bytes, and can be expected to benefit from the increased freedom of manoeuvre in certain circumstances. Apart from this, the potential performance will be slightly diminished on account of the reduced amount of primary storage.

The success of paging on a conventional machine such as the ICT Atlas depends on being able to present a virtual memory of such length that reorganisation is never necessary. Thus the Atlas location number of 24 bits allows for a conceptual store of 4096 pages of 4096 bytes (characters), one half of which give direct access to resident system routines, and the remainder are made available to each program by assigning to each a separate page table. The General Electric 645, which allows segmenting as well as paging, provides 36 address bits. Although the same principles could be applied on a codeword machine there must clearly be a point at which the cost of storing and maintaining virtual page tables outgrows the evil they are designed to avoid, i.e. store reorganisation, and for this reason it is improbable that one would make use of a page table very much larger than that determined by the physical storage on a Basic Machine. It will also be noticed that the paging system proposed above needs no extra fast storage beyond the ten bits used by the page address in each register, and no associative selection mechanism is required. Addressing is always direct except when crossing a page boundary.

In all paged systems a certain amount of store is wasted by rounding up each unit of the next integral number of pages, and this can be reduced by choosing small pages. However, the effect of this is to increase the 'boundary' effects (whichever paging scheme is used) and to increase the overhead costs of organising transfers to and from secondary storage. In the Basic Machine, it is not necessary for small blocks to participate in the paging scheme, and we can envisage a way round the dilemma in which a comfortably large page size is chosen to handle perhaps 80% of primary storage, the rest being occupied by subpage sets of data, codewords, chain elements, etc. whose allocation can be handled separately. In this way one would hope to achieve efficient use of high-speed primary storage without belabouring the page table or the secondary store control system.

5.3 Absorption

Pursuing the assumption that structural information confers no material benefits in developing or running programs, we may consider the steps necessary to reduce a program to linear form when no structural variation occurs. There is no difficulty in representing any part of the program tree in a single block, using relative codewords, though one may have to invent a codeword representation with a

71

bigger range than that given in Chapter 3. Local compound names such as 'h.3.0' can always be evaluated by the assembler and expressed directly as XC-relative addresses, so there will be some shortening of address paths when large agglomerations of instructions are formed. But it is unlikely that relative codewords could be entirely eliminated by such techniques, without affecting Basic Language, or that there would be any benefit from doing so, since the information they contain is already compactly stored and efficiently handled.

There remain to be considered the process base itself and the various special functions normally triggered by absolute codewords. If the base is placed contiguously with the program area then it is natural for XD to assume the role of a datum-limit word for the resulting block of store, which might be arranged as follows:

1. Registers (128 bytes)
2. Extended register store
3. Program area
4. Register stack

Local addresses held in the process base would be held in relative form and automatically modified by XD when used, and would thus be free from attention by store control routines. References to other programs would still be held in absolute form and require updating on reorganisation.

The two absolute codeword escapes which are not allowed in relative form are tag 1(5) lock-out, and tag 1(6) backing store reference. The former could be handled by the file and process control routines, but the latter could not, since it contradicts the assumption of invariant structure in the program area.

It is important to consider how the character of the system is changed by the above transformations, and we may refer back to the summary at the end of Chapter 1 for this purpose (p. 14). Since structure is still retained in the form of relative codewords, tags and type codes, the benefit of exact representation is preserved, and programs can still be said to be well oriented to that class of problems whose space requirements can be predicted before execution begins. Concealment of non-numerical coding is preserved, but the full benefits of integration with the operating system are lost because of the rigid store structure, which also makes it unlikely that any advances in technique would materialise. Running costs are not likely to change appreciably, but store allocation overheads could be reduced by having to deal with only one block for each process, though the benefits are likely to be shortlived in the presence of a backing store. Finally, in Basic Language itself there is very little change apart from the disappearance of **EQU**, **INSERT**, and **CIS**. The restrictions affecting tags must remain as long as address and instruction concealment is wanted.

5.4 Extensions

It is appropriate to conclude a description of the conservative aspects of the Basic Language Machine with a brief review of some immediate extensions.

Multilength data

The proposed register size of 64 bits is determined by the need for high-precision numerical calculation. In certain circumstances it might be justifiable to increase the size to admit even higher precision working, but in general this would only lead to wastage of space in the registers and process base as a whole, since all elements of mixed type must be rounded up to the largest size. Another approach, valid for both scientific and commercial data, is to treat entire sequences as single operands of the arithmetic functions by introducing distinctive type codes. For example, if type 16 describes a 4-bit decimal digit in a standard format, then an address with tag $2(16)$ and limit m would describe a number of $m + 1$ digits. Addition of two such numbers **X1, X2** is programmed simply by:

$$\textbf{X1} \quad \textbf{ADD} \quad \textbf{X2}$$

It is interpreted serially, one component at a time. Similarly, a multilength field comparison is afforded by **SUB*** (one must take the precaution of ensuring that byte sequences (character strings) compare correctly for collating purposes).

The addressing functions operate on multilength sequences to form subsequences in the normal way, and to convert the type description to multilength and back by means of **TAG**. Note that a 'singular multilength' quantity can be treated as a standard single-length item.

Declarative statements

Structural information which cannot be directly represented is normally conveyed by means of declarative statements, whose contents are absorbed in the process of generating instructions. In a conventional machine, type and set structure are handled in this way, while in the BLM they are recognised by hardware. There are several outstanding situations where such techniques are likely to be used in the Basic Language, particularly relevant to the interpretation of identifiers. In one of these, an identifier is expanded into a string of terms in the input text as the result of a declaration of the form:

$$\textbf{LET} \quad \alpha = \Sigma$$

where α is the identifier and Σ the formal expansion. For example, the elements of a set might be identified by:

$$\textbf{LET} \quad \textbf{A} = \textbf{k.0}$$
$$\textbf{LET} \quad \textbf{B} = \textbf{k.1}$$

etc. Thus **A**, **B** and so on could validly appear in any context permitting the use of compound names. A more compact expression of such relationships can be found, as in the example:

$$\textbf{LET} \quad \textbf{k} = (\textbf{A, B, C, D})$$

In conjunction with variable and constant set declarations, this sort of statement permits the assembler to apply the short cuts appropriate to a rigidly mapped store area. The constant expansion may be generalised to parametric form in various ways, one of the most obvious being a macro-function definition allowing for the introduction of user-defined 'machine functions'.

A declarative scheme requires complete structural information to be available at assembly time, and is therefore better applied to local names than globals. For example, we may seek to integrate the file and program stores by means of a 'type' declaration:

$$\textbf{FILE} \quad \textbf{F, G, H}$$

which identifies the file addresses, and allows the assembler to insert file control functions in place of addressing functions applied to the given variables. However, there is no proof against copying a file address into any other base position, and the only safe way to effect such a scheme is by dynamic interpretation of tag 1(7) elements.

Expressions

Another sort of expansion is afforded by the introduction of the binary infix operators $(+, -, *, /)$ corresponding to **ADD, SUB, MPY** and **DIV**, and the formation of expressions according to the usual arithmetic rules of precedence. The atomic terms in such expressions are constant or compound names which, as we have already noted, are themselves candidates for generalisation. An expression is assumed to be evaluated when the point at which it occurs in the program store hierarchy is accessed. It is legitimate in this context to generalise the notion of 'evaluation' to allow various formal transformations to be carried out.

One of the consequences of protecting instructions is that the complement of central registers can be distributed between different system components in an optimal manner. The division made in Chapter 3 is not necessarily permanent, and XA, XB, ..., XF can be used differently since they do not appear in the Basic Language at all. If extensive use is made of algebraic formalism, one can envisage more central registers being taken for special purposes, together with the introduction of inbred functions at Basic Machine level, while preserving the form of the Language. The actual number of 'hard' registers remains to be determined at any time by system and programming economics.

Evaluation

We have again encountered a situation in which, provided a structure is displayed to the assembly program, it can be absorbed into generated code without difficulty. If the expression is not known when writing code, one would usually arrange a jump to a subroutine to be supplied later. But it may not be known that an *expression* is required until after the code has been written. This is true of all global variables, and parameters in particular, which may be defined by numerical values, addresses, null elements, or by formulae which are to be evaluated dynamically. The escape trap on the Basic Machine provides the essential mechanism for handling such situations efficiently without the inconvenience of parameter 'type' declarations.

From what might be called the naïve method of translating expressions we can therefore predict evolution in two directions: first, towards partially or totally delayed evaluation permitting expressions to be transformed and evaluated dynamically, and second in the opposite direction, in which expressions are partially or totally evaluated by the assembly program using constant information in order to achieve more efficient code. A consistent display of this continuous spectrum of evaluation is the next major step in the development of Basic Language.

REFERENCES

[1] Burks, A. W., Goldstine, H. H., and von Neumann, J., 'Preliminary discussion of the logical design of an electronic computing instrument' (1946). See von Neumann, J., *Collected Works*, Vol. 5, pp. 34–79 (Pergamon 1961).

[2] Goldstine, H. H., and von Neumann, J., 'On the principles of large scale computing machines', (1946). See von Neumann, J., *Collected Works*, Vol. 5, pp. 1–33 (Pergamon 1961).

[3] 'The Descriptor', (Burroughs Corporation 1961).

[4] Iliffe, J. K., and Jodeit, Jane G. 'A dynamic storage allocation scheme', *Computer J.*, Vol. 5, p. 200 (1962).

[5] 'FORTRAN vs Basic FORTRAN', *Commun. Assoc. Comput. Mach.*, Vol. 7, pp. 591–624 (1964). (See Section 7.2.1.1.1.)

[6] Foster, J. M., *List processing* (Macdonald 1967).

[7] Iliffe, J. K., 'The use of the Genie system in numeral calculation', *Annual Review in Automatic Programming*, Vol. 2, pp. 1–28 (Pergamon 1961).

[8] Wirth, N., and Weber, H., 'EULER: A Generalization of ALGOL, and its Formal Definition: Part II', *Commun. Assoc. Comput. Mach.*, Vol. 9, pp. 89–99 (1966).

[9] Roos, D., *ICES System Design*, (MIT Press 1966).

[10] *SPAN*, NCR Elliott 4100 Programming Information, Part 3, Section 3 (1966).

[11] Gimble, E. P., 'Joss: Problem solving for engineers' RAND memorandum RM–5322–PR (1967).

[12] Dennis, J. B., 'Segmenting and the design of multiprogrammed computer systems', *1965 IEEE International Convention Record*, Part 3, pp. 214–225.

[13] Kilburn, T., 'One-level storage system', *IRE Transactions on Electronic Computers*, Vol. EC–11, No. 2 (April 1962).

[14] Daley, R. C., and Neumann, P. G., 'A general purpose file system for secondary storage', *Proceedings of the Fall Joint Computer Conference 27* (Spartan 1965).

APPENDIX

The language presented in Chapter 4 is based on the following classes of terminal elements:

Description	Class identifier	Definition
Function name	θ	see Table 5
Register name	χ	$\langle \mathbf{X0}|\mathbf{X1}|\ldots|\mathbf{X9}\rangle$
Integers	μ	$\langle \mathbf{0}|\mathbf{1}|\mathbf{2}|\ldots etc.\rangle$
Condition mnemonics	γ	see Table 4
Identifier—1	δ_1	$\langle \mathbf{A}|\mathbf{B}\ldots|\mathbf{Z}\rangle$
Identifier—2	δ_2	$\langle \mathbf{a}|\mathbf{b}|\ldots|\mathbf{z}\rangle$
Null element	Ω	undefined

The following constant symbols are used autonymously:

Dot	.	Entry point	#
Colon	:	Test variant	*
Parentheses	( )	;	
Comma	,		
Minus	—		

Also, the symbol ε is used to denote a blank position and ; for 'newline' in the formal definition.

Hence we derive the following classes:

Global name	β	$\langle \chi|\delta_1\rangle$
Local name	α	$\langle \delta_2|\#\mu\rangle$
Signed integer	μ_S	$\langle \mu|-\mu\rangle$
Global compound name	η_2	$\langle \beta|\eta_2.\mu\rangle$
Local compound name	η_1	$\langle \alpha|\eta_1.\mu\rangle$
Compound name	η	$\langle \eta_1|\eta_2|\Omega\rangle$
General argument	κ	$\langle \sigma|\eta\rangle$

The forms of file names ϕ and process names π are not defined, but would normally be represented as byte sets. If λ is any class identifier, then we define:

List	λ-list	$\langle \lambda|\lambda\text{-list},\lambda\rangle$

Hence:

Constant	σ	$\langle \sigma_0|\sigma_1|\sigma_2|\mu_S\rangle$
Zero set	σ_0	$[\mu\langle:|;\rangle\mu]$
Constant set	σ_1	$(\mu_S\text{-list})$
Constant name set	σ_2	$(\eta_1\text{-list})$

The functions fall into several classes, depending on the function identifier θ (see Table 5). They are listed as Formats 1–9, and defined as follows:

Instruction	ω	$\langle\omega_1|\omega_2|\omega_3|\omega_4|\omega_5|\omega_6|\omega_7|\omega_8|\omega_9\rangle$
	ω_1	$\eta\theta\kappa$
	ω_2	$\beta\theta\langle\eta|\mu\rangle$
	ω_3	$\beta\theta\beta$
	ω_4	$\beta\theta\kappa$
	ω_5	$\theta\ \kappa$-list
	ω_6	$\eta\theta\beta$
	ω_7	$\langle\beta|\varepsilon|\mu|\gamma\rangle\theta\kappa$
	ω_8	$\theta\mu$
	ω_9	$\theta\ \beta$-list

It is to be understood that where condition codes may be affected the function identifier θ may be replaced by $\theta*$ in the above formats to provide the 'test only' variant.

The program text definition is completed by:

Line	ρ	$\langle\rho_1|\rho_2\rangle$
Code	ρ_1	$\langle\eta_1:|\varepsilon\rangle\omega$
Constant	ρ_2	$\eta_1:\sigma$
Indirect text	τ_1	$\mathbf{SEG}\mu;\rho;\rho;\ldots;\rho;\mathbf{END}$
Direct text	τ_2	$\mathbf{CIS};\langle\tau_1|\omega\rangle;\langle\tau_1|\omega\rangle;\ldots$
		$\ldots\langle\tau_1|\omega\rangle;\mathbf{END}$

TABLES

Table 1: Tag codes (g)

Tag	Meaning
0	32-bit binary word
1	escape code (null element)
2	45-bit address
3	61-bit numeric

Table 2: Type codes (t) and sizes

Type	Meaning	Size (bits)
0	Binary word	32
1	Byte	8
2	Binary word (read-only)	32
3	Byte (read-only)	8
4	Instruction (mode 0)	32
5	Instruction (mode 1)	32
6	Instruction (mode 2)	32
7	Instruction (mode 3)	32
8	Absolute codeword	32
9	Relative codeword	32
10	Mixed type	64
11	Mixed type (read-only)	64
12	Long numeric	64
13	Short numeric	32
14	Long numeric (read-only)	64
15	Short numeric (read-only)	32

Table 3: Basic Machine functions

Mnemonic	Group	Result
ADD	A	$x + y$
AND	A	$x \wedge y$
COPY	B	Y
DIV	A	x/y
DOT	D	$X.y$
DUMP	B	Regs. to stack (N_{16})
INDEX	D	Limit (Y)
JUMP	C	Control transfer to y on condition N_4
JL	C	Jump if X last
JNL	C	Jump if X not last
JNT	C	Jump if not tracing
JPB	B	Jump to program base N_{16}
JSL	C	Jump and save link in X
JSM	C	Jump and set mark N_3
LDN	D	$-y$
LIM	D	Put limit y in X
LOAD	D	Value (Y)
LPB	B	Load program base address N_{16}
MEM	D	Index of X in Y
MOD	D	X modified by y
MON	C	Monitor code N_2
MOVE	A	y
MPY	A	$x * y$
NEQ	A	$x \not\equiv y$
NOT	A	$\ulcorner y$
OR	A	$x \vee y$
RET	C	Return to mark N_3
RF	B	Register fetch to X
RS	B	Register store from X
SCALE	A	$x * 2^y$
SHIFT	A	x shift by y logical
SIZE	A	Precision (y)
SUB	A	$x - y$
TEST	A	$x - y$: set cond. only
TTAG	D	Test tag $X{:}N_3$ or Read tag of Y to X
TTYPE	D	Test type $X{:}N_5$ or Read type of Y to X
UNDUMP	B	Stack to registers (N_{16})
WTAG	D	Write Tag $X = N_3$
WTYPE	D	Write Type $X = N_5$

Arguments

X	First argument register
Y	Second argument
x	First operand, by A/F
y	Second operand, by A/F
N_j	j-bit literal argument only

Table 4: Conditional jump mnemonics

Mnemonic	Test
GE	$\geqq 0$
GT	> 0
IR	Invalid result
LE	$\leqq 0$
LT	< 0
NZ	$\neq 0$
VR	Valid result
ZE	$= 0$

Table 5: Basic Language functions

Identifier	Group	Conditions	Format	Argument Tags	Meaning
ADD	A	*	1	Both N, by A/F	Arithmetic sum
AND	A	*	1	Both 0, by A/F	Logical product
CIS	E		3	1(9); 1(7)	Command input
COPY	B		4	Any	Copy tagged element
DIV	A	*	1	Both N, by A/F	Arithmetic quotient
DOT	D		2	2(C); 0 by A/F	Element selection
DUMP	B		5	Any	Arguments to stack
EQU	E		1	Any; 2(C)	Copy structure
INDEX	D	*	6	N; 2	Obtain limit value
INSERT	E		1	2; 0 by A/F	Insert elements in set
JL	C		4	2 or 0; 2(I)	Jump if last
JNL	C		4	2 or 0; 2(I)	Jump if not last
JUMP	C		7	Any; 2(I)	Jump (see p. 57)
LIM	D		2	2; 0 by A/F	Write limit value
LOAD	D	*	4	Any (see p. 44)	Evaluate
MEM	D	*	3	2; 2	Membership test
MOD	D		2	2; 0 by A/F	Modify address
MON	C		8	0 by A/F	Control monitor
MOVE	A	*	1	Both N, by A/F	Copy number
MPY	A	*	1	Both N, by A/F	Arithmetic product
NEQ	A	*	1	Both 0, by A/F	Logical difference
NOT	A	*	1	Both 0, by A/F	Logical complement
OPEN	E		4	Any; 2(2)	Open file
OR	A	*	1	Both 0, by A/F	Logical sum
PROC	E		4	Any; 2(2)	Start subprocess
RET	C		8	0	Return to link
RF	B		4	Any; 2(M)	Fetch tagged element
RS	B		4	Any; 2(M)	Store tagged element
SCALE	A	*	1	N; 0 by A/F	Arithmetic scale
SEG... ...END	E				Block assembly (i.e. indirect mode)
SHIFT	A	*	1	Both 0, by A/F	Logical shift
SIZE	A		1	0; N by A/F	Arithmetic precision
SUB	A	*	1	Both N, by A/F	Arithmetic difference
TAG	D	*	4	Any	Tag read or set
TFER	E		1	1(7), 2(2)	Input or output
TYPE	D	*	4	Any	Type read or set
UNDUMP	B		9	Any	Stack to base

83

Table 6: Escape codes

0 Undefined
1 Out of range
2 Indeterminate
3 Modification overflow
4 Cleared by program
5 Lock-out
6 Backing store address
7 File address
8 Soft interpretation
9 Process address

INDEX

Names of languages in capitals